The Hard Awakening

أَلَا يَا أَيُّهَا السَّاقِي أَدِرْ كَأْسًا وَنَاوِلْهَا

كَه عِشْق آسان نمود اوّل ولى أُفتاد مُشكِلها

حافظ

Love seemed at first an easy thing—
But ah! the hard awakening.

HAFIZ, *Love's Awakening*

The Hard Awakening

H. B. Dehqani-Tafti

Bishop in Iran
and President Bishop of the Episcopal Church
in Jerusalem and the Middle East

The Seabury Press · New York

1981
The Seabury Press
815 Second Avenue
New York, N.Y. 10017

First published 1981
Triangle
SPCK
Holy Trinity Church
Marylebone Road
London NW1 4DU

Printed in the United States of America

Library of Congress Cataloging in Publication Data

Dehqani-Tafti, H. B. (Hassan B.)
    The hard awakening.

    1. Iran—Politics and government—1979–
2. Dehqani-Tafti, H. B. (Hassan B.)
3. Anglican Communion—Bishops—Biography.
4. Bishops—Iran—Biography. I. Title.
DS318.8.D43 1981   955'.054'0924   81-1780
ISBN 0-8164-0496-8   AACR2

To Margaret, my wife,
who endangered her life for me,
and to the memory of
Bahram, our only son
who gave his life for both of us,
and for many more.

Contents

Preface

Ever since I wrote the short story of my life, *Design of My World*, over twenty years ago, friends have been urging me to write a sequel to it. Until now, there did not seem to be anything special to write about; and so nothing has been written.

The Iranian Revolution, and the events that followed, have had such an impact on my life, and all that I have lived and nearly died for, that I definitely have something to say now. Thank God we did not know from the beginning what was in store for us as a family and as a Church, otherwise I don't think we would have been able to bear it. The power to suffer hardship, persecution, and martyrdom was granted to us by God for each event as it happened, one after another, and we thank him for counting us worthy to witness to his love in our country and throughout the world.

In telling this story, however, which sometimes looks more like a fictional thriller than real life, I would like to make it perfectly clear that it is not my intention to denigrate my own country or its people in any way. Rather it is because I love my country and my people, and above all my small Church, that I am recording the things which happened to us:

For my country and its people, because I would like the people to know that freedom of religion is a very precious thing, so precious that a group of otherwise unimportant people were ready to risk everything for it. Yes, even in a Muslim country we have the intrinsic right to change our religion and become followers of Jesus Christ, and nothing should stop us from doing so. The atrocities which happened to us were the work of a small number of extreme fanatics, and not the policy of the government or the wish of the people as a whole. Certainly, the intellectuals had nothing to do with it, and they often admired us for standing up to persecution, and thus revealed the value of religious freedom.

For the world at large, particularly the Western world, so that they may not be under the illusion that man has progressed so much that suffering and persecution for one's faith is something of the ancient past. As long as human nature is what it is, and as long as there are sincere followers of the ways of God revealed in Jesus Christ, there will be persecution and martyrdom.

For our tiny Church in Iran, so that it may have a record of what happened to it at the time of its first testing. So that it may be assured of its real existence, because it was ready to stand and suffer rather than deny and give up. So that it may be sure of a continuing life, because it was ready to die.

H. B. Dehqani-Tafti, Bishop in Iran
Cambridge
November, 1980

1

The Gathering Storm

My first thought, as I stared up into the barrel of the revolver, was one of enormous relief. So this was death. It was over. At last, I was free of the intolerable strain of the past few months.

I hardly heard the shots—one doesn't, I am told, at that close range. Then I realized that I was still alive, and everything came floating back: the responsibilities, for the church and for my family, the administrative battles, the pastoral concerns. I was due to leave Iran in a few days' time, on church business. Would I now be able to go? Ought I to go? If I did, would I ever be able to return? I was aware of running footsteps. The assassins were making their escape, pursued, incredibly, by my wife Margaret. The whole episode had lasted only a few seconds.

Margaret returned, blood pouring from her left hand. There were immediate practical things to be done, like getting her to a hospital and phoning the police. We looked at the bed where we had been sleeping a short while before. On my pillow, a neat halo of four small holes encircled the place where my head had lain.

One thing was certain. This was not just a personal attack. It was the latest in a long series of violent incidents aimed at church members and property. Clearly they thought it was time to get rid of the Bishop.

The first intimations of possible trouble had come in the summer of 1978.

We were all together in England for a family reunion. I had travelled from Iran to attend the Lambeth Conference of Anglican bishops, accompanied by my wife Margaret and our youngest daughter, Guli. Sussanne, our second daughter, was already in London being trained as a nurse at St Thomas's Hospital; Shirin, the eldest, and our son Bahram, came over from America to join us. Shirin had been sent to Austin, Texas, two years before by Isfahan University, and she came back that summer with an M.A. in teaching English as a foreign language. Bahram also had spent two years in the United States. He was the pride of our family. His sisters adored him. His mother and I, who were naturally very proud of him, always wondered where he had got all his diverse talents from! He had just taken his M.A. degree in Economics at George Washington University, and this summer was to receive his B.A. from Oxford.

It was a very happy occasion. The ancient English universities of Cambridge and Oxford have always held an almost mystical fascination for me. I think I have regarded them with something of the same awe that my Muslim father reserved for Mecca! So it was with a good deal of emotion that I witnessed my son going through the ceremony of receiving his degree in the historic Sheldonian Theatre.

We were in the middle of the Lambeth Conference later that summer when sad and frightening news began to come out of Iran. We heard of riots almost daily in the cities. The television news showed scenes of uncontrolled demonstrations, shops and public places were attacked and looted, and, most horrifying of all, the Rex cinema in Abadan was set on fire and burned to the ground along with about 500 people trapped inside. The future for my country was looking very black indeed. It was clear that I ought to get back as soon as possible. So, on 4 September, with heavy hearts and much apprehension, we decided as a family to return to our country and our church, both of which we have served and loved all our lives.

Shirin had a job teaching English at Isfahan University, where she had been a student. She loved the work and was very much respected by both staff and students. Bahram had been taken on by the Oxford University

Press to work with the Iran Literature Association to promote their publications. He also had a second job, teaching economics and drama in one of the university colleges of Tehran. Sussanne stayed behind in England to finish her nursing training. Guli went back to school in Isfahan. Margaret and I settled in once again in the Bishop's House in Isfahan to do our best for the diocese which would obviously be facing difficult days ahead.

The day after we arrived in Isfahan martial law was declared in eleven towns, including Tehran and Isfahan. The following day, 8 September, came to be known as 'Black Friday', when demonstrators, ignoring the curfew, surged forward into machine-gun fire, so it was reported, and many people were killed. Obviously the movement, whatever it was, had gripped the country, and the central government seemed incapable of controlling it. Obviously, too, it was more than simply political. It was becoming apparent that the movement had the authority of religion behind it, and that the exiled Ayatollah Rouholla el Moossavy el Khomainy was the ruling force.

To understand the situation in Iran today it is necessary to go far back into the country's history.

There is a dichotomy within the Persian's soul. Deep down, he is a Persian, subconsciously aware of the glories of pre-Islamic Iran, and regarding the Arab conquest of his country in the seventh century AD as an unfortunate foreign invasion which wiped out the past glories of the Empire. But then a Persian is also almost always a Shi'a Muslim, giving thanks to Allah for the spread of the True Faith into Iran.

Psychologically, it is difficult for the two sides of his nature to meet peacefully, or ever to be completely reconciled. The uneasiness which has shown itself in the precarious balance of power between the religious leaders and the rulers of the country throughout its history stems from this uneasiness within the soul of its

3

citizens. Sometimes the religious leaders get the upper hand. Then the rulers have to listen to them. At other times the rulers seize power and try to subdue the religious leaders.

Ayatollah Khomainy upholds the Shi'ite doctrine that rulers must place themselves under the direction of the religious leaders. This doctrine he expounded in his book, symbolically entitled *Velayat-e Faqih*, or *The Authority of the Learned*, which was being widely distributed in the months preceding the Revolution. He supported his argument with quotations from the Qur'an, for example Surah 4:59: 'Oh! those who have believed obey God and obey His Messenger and those who have authority from them. Then if there is disagreement between you, pass it on to God and the Messenger.' He also quotes the Hadith as saying 'Truly the Ulama (the religiously learned) are the heirs of the prophets.' And again, 'The Ulama are rulers over the people' (alternatively, 'The Learned (Fuqaha) are rulers over kings').

Khomainy was always implacably opposed to Reza Shah, who had put an end to the rule of the Qajars and had been crowned as Shah of Iran in 1925. He denounced the Shah's policies of social reform, which followed the pattern of those of Kemal Attaturk in Turkey, maintaining that the religious leaders of the time ought to have stripped him of his powers. He vigorously condemned the further reforms of Muhammad Reza Shah who succeeded to the throne on the abdication of his father in 1940, and who promised to take his people into what he called 'the Great Civilization' within fifteen years. The young Shah's great mistake was that he was in too much of a hurry. True reform starts from within, and that takes a very long time. Unfortunately rulers cannot see this. In order to push through their reforms they become dictators, and dictators usually become aggressive.

Traditionally, the Crown of Persia has received its support from four areas: the landowning classes, the

4

tribes, the religious leaders, and, of course, the army. Muhammad Reza Shah sacrificed the support of the landowners by pushing through the land reforms. He forcibly subdued the tribes, thereby robbing himself of their support when he most needed it. The religious leaders disowned him because they regarded most of his reforms as anti-Islamic. So he was left to depend on the army, forgetting that the army, which was a conscript army, was made up of the people of the country, who belonged to the other three groups.

As always happens, too much power and wealth (in this case as a result of the increase in oil prices) drives out wisdom. A wise ruler ought ultimately to depend on his people. The Shah depended too much on his army, and the army was heavily dependent on the Americans.

In the early 1960s Ayatollah Khomainy, who was then teaching in the Faizieh Theological School in Qum, organized a demonstration against the Shah's land reforms. It was at his instigation that crowds were let loose in the streets of Tehran, causing a great deal of damage to public property. The Shah sent in his troops, and by sunset many people had been killed.

At this stage the Shah could have moved more slowly. Had he listened to the elders of the state, and replaced his young Prime Minister with an older man respected by the religious groups, he might have calmed the rebellion. Instead he got rid of the older men around him who were prepared to speak their minds, brought in younger ones who flattered him and did not dare oppose him and, worst blunder of all, sent the Ayatollah Khomainy into exile, first to Turkey and then to Iraq.

Now, sending an influential religious leader into exile may at first seem an easy way of getting rid of the trouble-maker, but in the long run it only gives him more influence and power than ever. Very soon Khomainy became the national figure who had stood up for God and religion against the powers of this world and had been sent into exile and unjustly treated on that account.

5

The more the SAVAK, the Shah's secret police, tried to wipe out Khomainy's influence, the more popular he became with the common man. His picture was seen hanging in the houses of the poor and in smaller shops throughout the country.

But Khomainy could not have brought about the Revolution alone. He needed the co-operation of the intellectuals and the middle classes, and he got it. This group more than any other hated the oppression of the Shah's regime, particularly the power of the SAVAK. Being few in number, they could not have succeeded by themselves, so they rallied round Khomainy.

The alliance created a formidable power, both outside the country in the capital cities of the West, and inside Iran through their underground activities. Most of the intellectuals perhaps did not care much about religion, but they knew well that religion can be a rallying point, so gave their support to the movement. Among this group were political leaders of the old National Front which a quarter of a century before had brought Dr Mussadeq to power: Dr Sanjabi, Dr Seddiqi, Dr Bakhtiar, and Dr Matin-Daftari. There were poets and writers, such as Mahmood Inayat, Hajsaid Javady, Shamoloo, and Akhaven-e Saless. But there were also some intellectuals who were intensely religious. The most famous of these, who did not live to see the Revolution come to fruition but had perhaps done more than anybody else to bring it about, was Dr Ali Shariaty.

He already had a deep faith in Shi'ite Islam when he went to the Sorbonne to study sociology. His writings, *Tashy'oe Alavy va Tasy'oe Safavy* (Shi'ism according to Ali and Shi'ism according to Safavids) and *Dar Rah e Shenakht-e Islam* (In the Way of Knowing Islam) show evidence of his encounter with modern revolutionary theories, including Liberation Theology. These he very ably managed to adapt to the Shi'ite doctrine of martyrdom and of suffering for truth's sake as seen in the tragedy of Karbala, where Imam Hussain, the son of Ali (son-in-law of the Prophet), gave his life in fighting for truth, knowing that he would be martyred. His rhetorical description of this event is so moving that it strikes a chord in the heart of any Iranian, even the most indifferent.

Like most scholars, Shariaty was not physically very strong. His struggle with the SAVAK did not help his health. While his writings were being read by intellectuals, both religious and agnostic, throughout Iran, and while the foundations of the Revolution were being prepared, he died in a London hospital. Rumours began circulating that he had been mysteriously murdered by the SAVAK, and he was soon regarded as a martyr.

One of the characteristics of pre-revolutionary days, which has continued to this day, is the role played by rumour. Most people seem to accept a bad rumour the moment they hear it, and pass it on, adding something to it on the way. No one asks for tangible proofs. Nobody questioned how it was possible for Dr Shariaty to have been murdered in a London hospital without the police making enquiries, or the news media raising disturbing questions. Anybody who expressed such doubts would have been regarded as anti-revolutionary and pro-government.

While radio and television, newspapers and magazines, and the printing of books were under the careful control of the SAVAK, it proved impossible to control the mosques. There are thousands of them all over the country. They provided a marvellous network for inculcating Khomainy's revolutionary ideas, which poured into the country by means of cassettes and photocopies—so-called 'night letters'. The messages were simple enough, and would not have had such an impact had it not been for the oppression of the SAVAK, who would use the slightest sign of opposition as a reason for making an arrest. Even an ordinary invitation card for our church services had to be checked and scrutinized by the SAVAK; and if the name of the Shah was mentioned anywhere, the right adjectives would have to be added before it.

In such an atmosphere, listening to a religious leader telling you that 'All the evils of our country are the work of this father and this son' (meaning Reza Shah and Muhammad Reza Shah); or 'Our agriculture has suffered because Muhammad Reza has sold himself and our country to the Americans, to give them our oil money and store up their useless metals' (meaning arms)—this kind of talk very easily moved the listeners to oppose all the policies of the Shah, and all the government's efforts at reform.

Apart from arson and acts of terrorism in the towns, strikes and demonstrations became the order of the day. The most astute move that Khomainy made, from his point of view, was to leave Iraq for Paris. In Europe he had at his disposal the entire mass media of the world. No longer did we hear by rumour only that there was to be a general strike: the BBC Persian programme, to which nearly everyone listened, would tell us that! So much so, that people who did not understand the workings of the Western media came to believe that because the BBC gave detailed news about Ayatollah Khomainy, sometimes with a bias against the Shah, therefore the British Government was behind the Revolution.

One of the most unfortunate characteristics of us Iranian people is our lack of a sense of responsibility for our destiny. Very few of us believe that, apart from acts of God, our destiny can be in our own hands. As a result of a long history of foreign interference in Iranian affairs, we still suppose that everything is engineered either by the British, the Russians, or the Americans. That is why in times of crisis the people become indecisive and easily manipulated. We do not believe that we can influence affairs in any way. We wait to see how the great powers, depending on which

8

one we think is mysteriously running things, will act. So events are allowed to drift on, and are finally moulded by the few who have outgrown this nineteenth-century dream. My son Bahram, who saw the dangers of this frame of mind, wrote an article for a Tehran English magazine of those days, *The Iranian* (31 October, 1979). He called it 'Limits to Imperialism; Our Lives in our Hands', and ended it by saying:

> Pure apathy is, at least, intellectually excusable, because nationalism cannot be force fed. But continually to shift the blame for our deficiencies on to foreigners is not only indefensible but dangerous. There could not be a state of mind more conducive to those foreign powers that do wish to influence our future.

The forces behind the Revolution did not seem to have any doubt as to who was pushing them: Ayatollah Khomainy, with his indomitable politico-religious ideas, having gathered around himself intellectuals from both right and left.

An important religious and social custom in Iran is the commemoration of the dead. The third, seventh, and fortieth days after a death, besides the successive anniversaries, are occasions for special observance. These provided a marvellous opportunity for the revolutionaries. As events proceeded, the number of martyrs multiplied. So there were ample reasons for declaring commemoration days of public mourning for various individuals, or groups of martyrs. When a day was declared a 'closing day', life came to a standstill. On 10 November I was in Yazd, a town of about 300,000 population, 400 miles south of Tehran. I had a puncture and needed to change the tyre, but not a garage or repair shop was open. In the end someone told me I would find one outside the town on the road to Kerman. When I asked the owner how it was he had remained open, he explained, 'It is an order from the Aqa', meaning the local Ayatollah Saddooqi, who seemed to have the whole town in the palm of his hand. For the sake of travellers, 'the Aqa' had decreed that this shop, and one other on the north side of the town, should keep open for business. Clearly they were well organized.

More and more, the walls of the towns were becoming covered with slogans: pro-Khomainy, anti-Shah, anti-American, anti-West. The most popular slogan was 'Freedom, Independence, Islamic republic'—freedom from the oppression of the Shah; independence from foreign influences; and an Islamic republic, not a monarchical and secular government.

It was not quite clear at this stage of affairs what was meant by an 'Islamic republic'. However, it was noticeable that the tone of the movement was becoming increasingly Islamic, using Qur'anic terminologies and depicting Shi'ite prototype figures symbolizing good and evil. During curfew hours, when people were not allowed out in the streets, families would go on to the rooftops and chant the old Islamic battle-cry, *'Allahu Akbar*—God is Greater.' Some of the catch phrases at the time cleverly utilized the Persian love of rhyme— *'Allahu Akbar! Khomainy Rahbar!*—God is greater, Khomainy is leader!'

Though the tone was definitely Islamic, the religious minorities were not forgotten. At Christmas time a printed bulletin from Imam Khomainy and addressed to Christians was pushed through our door, reminding Christians of their long-standing close ties with Islam, and asking them to rise against oppression. So we felt reassured that under an Islamic regime our rights would be preserved.

Meanwhile chaos was increasing daily. Strikes were commonplace. Postal strikes lasted for weeks at a time. There were blackouts because of power cuts. Rumours of impending scarcities of kerosene, petrol, and bread

10

frightened people and led to hoarding.

On 4 November the civilian government of Mr Sharif Imami fell, and General Azhary took over; the sound of gunfire increased by day and at night. We stuck by our television sets for news, and most people listened to the BBC Persian broadcasts on their radios. We saw pictures of well-organized demonstrations in Tehran led by National Front leaders such as Dr Sanjabi, Dr Matin-Daftari, and Dr Bakhtiar. The BBC would tell us that on such and such a day about a million people had walked in orderly fashion from one point in Tehran to another, shouting slogans against the Shah and against America. The same sort of thing—though on a smaller scale—happened in Isfahan and other towns.

11 December 1978 coincided that year with the day of Ashura. This is the day when Shi'ites everywhere commemorate the martyrdom of Imam Hussain. It is marked with flagellation and chest-beating and other modes of mourning such as were prevalent in some Christian countries in the Middle Ages. Religious fervour and fanatical emotions can be so worked up that people will accept martyrdom as a welcome gift.

For me, that day marked the turning point of the movement towards Revolution. Crowds gathered round the statues of the Shah in nearly every town and pulled them down. Even the awesome SAVAK headquarters in Isfahan was attacked. It was becoming increasingly obvious who was controlling events. A few months earlier you could not have said one word against the Shah, and now his statue, and that of his father, was being toppled, and seemingly no one could do anything to stop it.

Two days later the martial law commander of Isfahan, General Naji, organized a pro-Shah demonstration in the city, but it failed. A month later, almost exactly to the day, he was captured by the revolutionaries and three days later was executed in Tehran with three other generals.

By the end of December the whole of the oil industry had come to a standstill as the result of a general strike. We had large English-speaking congregations in Tehran, Ahwaz, and Isfahan. As the expatriates left the country, the number of those attending our church services also dramatically decreased. It was at this time that our chaplain in the oilfields left because he did not have anyone to minister to. In Isfahan there was a large American contingent teaching the Iranian Air Force the art of flying helicopters. Many of them were members of St Luke's Church, where at that time the Reverend Paul Hunt, a missionary of the Church Missionary Society, was responsible for the English-speaking services. The congregation had a good choir, and they just managed to put on a performance of the *Messiah* before Christmas. Within a week they had all left. One Sunday the church was full, the next only about eight people were worshipping together in the English language, though Persian services continued as usual, under the pastoral care of the Reverend Iraj Mutta-heddeh.

Amidst increasing tension and many contradictory rumours General Azhary resigned, and Dr Shahpour Bakhtiar was appointed Prime Minister on 6 January 1979. The Shah and Queen Farah left Tehran ten days later. Khomainy declared his opposition to Bakhtiar on the grounds that he had been appointed by the Shah.

Dr Bakhtiar tried to postpone the return of Kho-mainy, but was not successful. Ayatollah Khomainy returned victoriously to Tehran on 1 February 1979. One small incident probably passed unnoticed by many, but sent shivers down the spines of some who watched on television his triumphant return. When the aeroplane reached Iranian airspace and neared Tehran, one of the reporters travelling with the Aya-tollah approached him reverently and asked him through an interpreter what were his feelings on returning to

12

his country after fifteen years of exile.

'Nothing,' the Ayatollah replied indifferently. 'Nothing at all.'

On 6 February a BBC television team including Harold Briley and John Simpson, who were filming in Isfahan, interviewed me and filmed some of our church activities. They told me that as far as they could tell the revolutionaries had won and Isfahan was already in their hands. But the army was still in evidence everywhere, with tanks at every crossroads and sentries standing guard with machine guns.

We had decided to close down the two small hostels we ran for boys and girls, as we were running out of supplies of food and kerosene. Four of the missionaries in charge of the hostels were to leave Isfahan for Tehran on the 11th.

On Saturday, the 10th, in the evening, there was suddenly an unusual call from the small mosque opposite the Bishop's House in Abbas-Abad Avenue. Normally the *muezzin* intones the *azan*, the call to prayer, or recites the Qur'an. This time it was a strange voice, apparently of a young man, and speaking rather than intoning, in an Isfahani accent: 'We have had news from Tehran. Be prepared. When you hear the sign do not go and hide inside your rooms, come out of your houses.' It sounded ominous. I telephoned our church representatives in Tehran to ask if it would be safe for the missionaries, one of them a pregnant woman, to travel to the capital. They emphatically advised against it. The next day, Sunday 11 February, the army was recalled to barracks. The revolutionaries broke into the arsenals and helped themselves to firearms. Dr Bakhtiar disappeared, and for a long time no one knew where he was.

The Majlis, the Iranian Parliament, was dissolved by Khomainy. Mr Bazargan, a Muslim intellectual, was appointed by him as Prime Minister. So the Ayatollah and his followers had won.

Most people sincerely believed that the country would now be free from dictatorship and oppression. Many organizations and institutions sent their congratulations, and pledged their support. I too sent a letter on behalf of the Diocese of Iran to Khomainy and to the new government in Tehran, declaring our co-operation with the aims of the Revolution, and praying God for the establishment of freedom and justice in our country.

2

Iran and Western Missionaries

The history of Christianity in Iran goes back to the Acts of the Apostles when, on the Day of Pentecost, Parthians and Medes were among the crowds in Jerusalem who listened to Peter's preaching. To go back even earlier, there is an ancient tradition that the Wise Men who brought gifts to the infant Jesus originated from Hamedan or Saveh, in Persia! Later, St Thomas may have passed through Persia on his way to evangelize India. Another strong tradition tells us that Simon the Zealot brought the gospel to Iran. Certainly, as far as historical records are concerned, there was an organized church in the country by the second century.

So when the armies of Islam invaded Iran in the seventh century, there were already established churches there, whose presence was tolerated by the new Muslim rulers, along with that of Jews and Zoroastrians, though under conditions which made them in effect second-class citizens. Their fate down the centuries has largely depended on the attitude of the ruler of the day, and the relationship of that ruler with the religious leaders.

These ancient religious minority groups have survived until the present day, protected by the Muslims, with their own special identity, free to live and worship according to their own traditions, always provided they do not attempt to make converts from among the Muslims. In fact, there is a sense in which these religious minorities have enjoyed more freedom than the Muslims themselves. A Muslim is forbidden to change his religion, whereas a Jew, a Zoroastrian, or a Christian is free to do so.

This state of affairs has been taken for granted for centuries, with the result that the religious minorities

15

have withdrawn very much into themselves. To be a Muslim was synonymous with being an Iranian, while a Christian, ethnically and by reason of his religion, was a 'foreigner', Assyrian, or Armenian, protected by the House of Islam so long as he remained obedient to Islamic law.

This was the situation when the Englishman Henry Martyn translated the New Testament into Persian at the beginning of the nineteenth century. It was perhaps symbolic that when Henry Martyn wished to present his work to Fat'hali Shah, the ruler of the day, he had to do it through Sir Gore Ousely, the British Ambassador to the Court of the Shah. Thus from the start Christianity in its modern aspect was identified with a foreign government.

When, later in the century, in the period of great missionary expansion, British and American missionaries entered the country, they lived at first among the Assyrian and Armenian communities where they were pioneers in the fields of medicine and education, setting up hospitals and schools which were soon to become famous throughout the country.

In the early days resistance was shown to these missionary establishments by the religious leaders, particularly to the schools. Parents were forbidden to send their children to Christian schools; often students would climb over the walls because the doors were watched, knowing that they risked being caught and beaten. But as time went on the missionary institutions became accepted and increasingly used by the people. Even religious leaders would call in missionary doctors for medical treatment. Occasionally Ayatollahs, and more often lesser religious dignitaries, would attend hospitals for surgery. Gradually even sons and daughters of religious leaders went to missionary schools and colleges for study.

It was out of these missionary activities that there grew the beginnings of an indigenous Iranian church.

16

But right from the start that church had the stigma of 'foreign-ness'. Just as Henry Martyn could not have presented his New Testament to Fat'hali Shah without the help of the British Ambassador of the day, so the American and British missionaries could not have built and run their hospitals and schools without the protection of their respective governments, particularly the prestige and influence of the British in the nineteenth century. Thus, ironically, the greatest obstacle in the way of the growth of the Church in Iran lay in the very cause of its existence.

It has become fashionable nowadays to denigrate missionaries and missionary movements, to identify them with Western imperialism, and even to condemn them for having existed at all. I cannot agree with these condemnations. I am convinced that the missionary movement of the Church of Christ, for all its many defects and faults, has done more good to mankind than any other single movement in history. The success or failure of the Christian mission is not to be judged in terms of political or material results, such as the introduction of heavy industry or the granting of huge loans. It is seen in the lives of innumerable individuals changed from selfishness to unselfish living, from ignorance to knowledge, from abject misery to the dignity of the sons of God.

Of course missionaries have made mistakes. Of course they have often been selfish, or wilful, or overtly proud of their own colour, culture, and country. But on the whole they have genuinely tried to represent their Lord in serving mankind. If their governments have been powerful in the world, this has not been of their doing. It is possible that sometimes governments have used missionaries to serve their policies; but it is also true that missionaries have been able to use the stability and security afforded by the power of their respective governments to spread the gospel and to build up their schools and hospitals, sometimes against the will of those very governments.

The missionary movement is not the product of the Western world. It started in the Middle East with Jesus Christ, himself the Sent One, who claimed: 'He has sent me to proclaim release for prisoners' (Luke 4.18), and who commanded his disciples to 'Go forth to every part of the world and proclaim the Good News to the whole creation' (Mark 16.15).

This the Church has been doing ever since, with the difference that in the first century Christian missionaries represented a small, poor, oppressed minority who carried their message to the most powerful and the richest state in the world, the Roman empire. In the nineteenth and twentieth centuries the situation has been reversed. Each age has had its problems. The message is the same. In neither situation did the missionaries recognize the right of governments to forbid the mission of the Church being expressed in action. It was not necessary for either to apologize for what they were. Both had to do their duty, and they did it.

The good things of life ought to be shared by all mankind. Aristotle, Plato, and Socrates were not imprisoned within the time and culture of ancient Greece, but have enriched all mankind. Aspects of Buddhism have influenced Muslim mysticism. Islamic thought and scientific achievements have greatly affected Western development. British ideas of democracy and justice have been adopted by many peoples throughout the world.

Christians have something of supreme importance to share with all mankind—their belief in the God of love who revealed himself in Jesus Christ who loved mankind to the extent of being ready to die for us without hate or resentment. They have proved that trusting such a God cleanses men from hate and suspicion, heals their inner wounds, and makes them whole. This is the Good News they long to share with

18

the rest of the world, and no one has the right to stop them. Islam sends its missionaries all over the world. Why should Christians lose their right to do so?

Of course, if you are afraid of the message which is going to change your society, and you hate any change because it upsets your vested interests, and you have no logical way to combat that message, you start to persecute and annihilate the messenger. So you call the messenger names, like 'imperialist', 'paternalist', 'foreign agent', or 'spy', so that people will hate him and forget his message. That is what the religious and political leaders of the day did to Jesus, and that is what the world is doing today to Christian missionaries.

Throughout the Middle East, ever since Lawrence of Arabia every English person, and nowadays every American, who speaks Arabic or Persian fluently is supposed to be a spy. Because missionaries normally give more time to the language and live longer among the people to whom they have gone, it is taken for granted that they are all spies! No one asks what there is to spy on in a small remote town or village, or why this espionage should make it necessary for large numbers of doctors, nurses, teachers, and pastors to live there for many years. It is time to expose this accusation against missionaries.

I nearly lost my life, and my only son was murdered, because we were Christians; and I and my family are Christians because men and women were ready to leave their country in the last century to preach the Christian Gospel to Iran.

After about fifty years of work by the Church Missionary Society the Anglican Diocese of Iran was officially established in 1912, with small churches in four towns in the south of the country, and with hospitals and schools in each of these towns, still mainly staffed by missionaries. In the early years it had to contend with the influence of the local *mujtahids*, or religious leaders.

19

On the whole these men, who wielded enormous power in the country, had come to accept the medical services of the church, but remained unfavourable to the educational establishments. With the coming of the Pahlavi dynasty the authority of the religious leaders waned, and the central government in Tehran became increasingly powerful. It was by Reza Shah's dictatorial order, which no one dared to oppose at the time, that the large and prestigious missionary schools and colleges were taken over by the government in 1940. Thus the church was deprived of all its educational institutions for the time being.

The nationalization of the Iranian oil industry by Dr Mussadeq in the early 1950s was another crucial time for the church, as well as for the country. Looking back now, I believe that the events of those days contained the seeds of the Khomainy Revolution, though no one foresaw that at the time. What has happened now, in the Revolution, had already started during what has come to be called the oil crisis. So far as the church was concerned, foreign missionaries who were outside the country at the time were not allowed back. The Anglican bishop of the time, the Right Reverend W. J. Thompson, who was a British citizen, was expelled. The Christian hospital in Isfahan was given six months' notice to close down. We had no option but to comply. Then Dr Mussadeq fell and the Shah, who had gone into exile, came back. The next day we were told by the Department of Health to begin accepting patients again.

Soon after the settlement of the oil dispute Bishop Thompson came back, and the church saw in his return another sign that it should carry on as before. Looking back nearly thirty years, it is easy to say that we ought to have read the writing on the wall and accommodated ourselves to the spirit which brought about the oil crisis. Instead, it seemed to us to be God's will that the hospital should remain in the hands of the church.

I am sure now that the right thing would have been somehow to have 'nationalized' our hospitals and indeed our other institutions. The American Presbyterians, who perhaps saw better the signs of the times, closed, handed over, or sold all their seven hospitals in the north of the country. We were reluctant to close down good and useful establishments, but we would have been wise to negotiate with the government or groups of interested doctors, and divest ourselves of the immense responsibilities of running these big organizations.

Of all our institutions, the hospitals were the most difficult to run. Most of the workers were non-Christians; there were not enough missionary or senior Christian staff to make them truly Christian establishments. We depended heavily on CMS to send us missionaries, but they had warned us a long time before that they might not always be able to send us enough workers. They made it clear that it was our responsibility to run the hospitals, or close them down, or hand them over, as we thought best. At every meeting of the Diocesan Medical Board, ever since the second world war, the problem of staffing had been foremost on the agenda. But the doctors in charge would rather have died of overwork than close down or hand over the hospitals.

In the first half century of its life, the diocese had had three missionary bishops. Bishop Thompson, the third of these, spent altogether about fifty years in the country, having come out originally to be headmaster of my old school, the Stuart Memorial College in Isfahan. He became bishop in 1935. In 1960 he announced his intention of retiring. Who was to succeed him as bishop of the diocese which was the smallest numerically, and perhaps the largest geographically, within the Anglican Communion?

Archbishop Campbell MacInnes of Jerusalem visited the diocese and went round the churches asking members for their views. Most of them wanted an Iranian bishop, but felt it was a bit too early. The Archbishop therefore wrote to the Diocesan Council, which was meeting to discuss the future, saying he had come to the conclusion that it would be best to invite a retired English bishop to come for two or three years as a caretaker, after which he would consecrate an Iranian, whom the church should elect. The Diocesan Council totally rejected this proposal and proceeded to elect an Iranian then and there. It happened to be me.

At the time, I had little idea what it meant to be the bishop of a Church such as ours. I knew only one thing: I had grown up in the Church, been nurtured in the Church, and was ready to do anything I could for the Church. I felt the truth of our Lord's words to his disciples in John 15.16: 'You did not choose me: I chose you. I appointed you to go on and bear fruit, fruit that shall last. . . .'

At that time I had no idea what the cost of this new 'appointment' would be. But I remember feeling very weak and inadequate for the job. This was not false humility. It was genuine lack of experience and knowledge. What was a bishop for? What would be involved in being a bishop in a tiny church in the midst of a population that was 99.5 per cent Muslim?

A friend kindly sent me a book called *The Bishop in the Church*. It was all very interesting, but hardly what I needed at the time. It was full of diagrams explaining the vestments and the movements a bishop must make when conducting services, but said nothing about the true meaning of the office. Several years later Bishop Howe, the Secretary-General of the Anglican Consultative Council, who visited us in Isfahan and with whom I talked about the subject, sent me a book containing essays by different writers, which was much more practical and a great help.

But now, as I was feeling very unprepared, weak, and inadequate for the job, there came to my mind the mysterious, seemingly paradoxical truth contained in the words, 'My grace is all you need; power comes to its full strength in weakness' (2 Cor. 12.9). Fear and uncertainty disappeared. I realized that I was qualified for the job simply because I thought I was not qualified. The power of God could work with me because I had no power of my own. His strength filled the vacuum of my own weakness.

And so I went to be consecrated in Jerusalem on St Mark's day, 25 April, 1961.

The enthronement ceremony in Isfahan a little later was a very happy occasion for our small community. St Luke's Church, in which I had been baptized, confirmed, made deacon, and married, and of which I had for many years been pastor, was packed with guests, Christians and non-Christians. I was accepted by my church as its fourth bishop with thanksgiving and jubilation. Our son Bahram, then about five, hearing somebody say that I was the fourth bishop replied 'But Daddy is the first Iranian bishop'.

3

The First Persian Bishop

I have explained that the tiny indigenous Iranian church slowly grew out of large missionary establishments, and for this reason the government officially recognized it as a foreign organization. They welcomed our charitable institutions. They even helped us financially sometimes. On the whole they closed their eyes to our religious activities. Preaching was allowed within our hospitals and blind schools, and of course no difficulty was raised over worship services in churches, whether in English or in Persian.

We wondered what the reaction would be when the first Persian bishop was appointed. In fact, the government of the day ignored the event completely, and in the country as a whole it went practically unnoticed. Only one national paper printed my photograph, with a short paragraph explaining that I was the first native Iranian to hold this position. A provincial paper which was owned by a fanatical Muslim group had a few mocking things to say. But that was all. The Christian community as a whole welcomed this new development, and the Presbyterians, the Roman Catholics, and the Armenians each sent representatives to the enthronement service.

During my nineteen years as bishop of the diocese I have enjoyed the love, loyalty, and co-operation of my team of clergy and other diocesan workers. There have, I admit, been times when I have not seen eye to eye with some of the more strong-minded missionaries, when I have felt that their way of running the hospitals was out-dated, or I have disagreed with their methods of evangelism. But on the whole we were content each to work in our separate ways.

The Anglican Church in Iran had always tried to

24

maintain relationships with Muslim society. Apart from contacts through our schools and hospitals, another way of making direct contact was the annual Christian Invitation service in St Luke's Church. Bishop Thompson had started the tradition of inviting leading figures from the city and government officials to an afternoon tea followed by a short service. I carried on this tradition, and was pleased to see that a good number of people responded. The short service included a sermon which had been allotted to me ever since I had been ordained a priest. So for about thirty years I had the opportunity of expounding the Christian faith to the intellectual and influential people of the city. I would spend a great deal of time preparing these sermons, for which I found Dr Kenneth Cragg's books on Christian-Muslim relationships extremely helpful. Many of these sermons were subsequently published in book form in Persian.

I thanked God that by this means I could reach the educated classes, and also gain acceptance in my own country as one who had come from a Muslim background to a position of authority in the Christian Church. For there was a sense in which my Persian origins were actually a handicap to my position, and therefore to some extent to the Church as a whole. I was never entirely at ease in Iranian society. By deciding for Christ when I was still a boy, I had cut myself off from my Muslim roots. Socially, I came from a poor village family, from whom I found myself distanced both educationally and culturally. My marriage to an Englishwoman, although as perfect as any marriage can be in this world, separated us still more from the normal Iranian society around us. In other words, I was a lonely man, with no means and with no influence in society, yet I carried the great responsibility of leading a church which needed all the influence it could find to safeguard its interests. Of course, it is true that ultimately it is God who cares for his Church, and indeed it was because I believed this so strongly that I answered his call and accepted the job. But still, when it came to practicalities like negotiating with government offices with regard to our institutions and properties, I often felt very weak indeed.

Two friends in particular were a tremendous help to me at this time, in their different ways.

The first was an American lady by the name of Mrs Abby Grey, who visited our home in Isfahan just before I was elected bishop. She was a wealthy lady and extremely keen on modern art. She visited the Middle East and India several times and finally established the Grey Art Gallery in New York. Abby Grey was one of those rare women who though very rich live very simply. As an Episcopalian—her brother was a priest in New York—she took an interest in the problems of our church, and was endowed with the kind of imagination that could enter into another person's world and bring all the sympathy possible with it. She was a copious letter writer and over the years our correspondence grew. We had many disagreements, but though I fear I was often rude to her in defending what I thought to be my position, she never for one moment swerved from her sympathy towards me, my family, and my work.

One of the things Abby Grey did for us was to give us a garden to which we could go for quiet whenever we needed to be on our own. This gift proved to be vital for the spiritual health, not only of myself and my family but of the church as a whole. The Bishop's House where we lived was part of a large and busy compound which also contained the vicarage, St Luke's church and the hospital, so we as a family were never on our own. Even the diocesan offices were part of the Bishop's House. Abby Grey saw the need of a separate place long before I saw it myself. We called the place 'Abby Garden' and built a small cottage there. It became a haven not only for myself and the family:

missionaries who needed quiet often used it. Several times we held retreats there for clergy and others.

Besides, owning a piece of land has a curious effect on a person. It gives one a sense of belonging—something which I had needed very badly without knowing it. Humanly speaking, I had felt cut off from my own people in the deepest things of life. Whenever I visited Taft, my home village, it gave me a queer feeling of belonging and yet not belonging. I was of the soil of the place, and yet I felt very strange to it. In Abby Garden this feeling was resolved. I was liberated from my state of 'nonbelongingness' to the soil. It was a wonderful sensation. It gave me a kind of invisible inner dignity. The experience of Abby Garden has convinced me that every human being ought to be able to have a corner in this world that he can call 'mine'!

Maybe saints can transcend this materialistic need. But it is very difficult to transcend from a vacuum. I remember reading many years ago a book called *I Leap Over the Wall* by Monica Baldwin. The writer, who had been a nun for many years, expressed much the same kind of feeling when she left the convent and found a house of her own.

Another close friend without whose help, support, and advice I could not have carried my responsibilities was John McDouall, a lay member of our church. His grandfather had come to the Persian Gulf area from Scotland, and John is very proud of his Scottish heritage. At the same time he is very Persian in his ways. He seems to combine the good qualities of the Scottish character with the best of the Persian qualities, with wonderful results. Any difficulties which came my way he seemed able to solve gently and quietly. He lost a great deal as a consequence of the Revolution, and the diocese remains very much indebted to him.

One of my first priorities on becoming bishop was to develop our church's educational programme. Before his retirement Bishop Thompson had established two diocesan primary schools, for boys and girls respectively. I have always had a particular interest in the field of education, and establishing a boarding school like the old Stuart Memorial College was the dream of my life. So the first years of my service as bishop were spent in founding such an institution.

Haj Mussavarul Mulk, the renowned miniaturist, who was a staunch supporter and friend of the old college, granted a large plot of land for the purpose just outside Isfahan. A legacy to the diocese from another well-wisher enabled us to buy some more land, so that we had enough to build a school, boarding houses, and several homes for the headmaster and staff, as well as playing fields, including a football pitch. Through the World Council of Churches, the German Evangelical Agency came to our help and paid for the whole building project. A Persian Christian was accepted by the government as headmaster. The CMS promised to send two full-time missionaries and a few short-term teachers, and the project got off the ground. A dream had been realized. Within a few years the Carr Boarding School came to be one of the best secondary schools in the country. Alongside this project, a secondary school for girls was also developed under the headship of Miss Mary Isaac. Within the first decade of my service as bishop, the diocese had educational facilities for boys and girls from kindergarten up to university entrance.

Besides the ordinary schools, we had come to be responsible for the biggest and best organization for blind welfare in the country, including two schools for blind pupils. This work had been originated by a German Christian, Ernst Christoffel, who opened the first home for blind children in Isfahan in the 1920s. I remember as a schoolboy of fifteen going to teach there. Then the second world war broke out, and in 1941 after Allied armies had occupied Iran, Pastor Christoffel was interned and deported by the British, leaving his mission orphaned overnight. It thus became the responsibility of the diocese. It took Bishop Thompson two years to find the right person to run it. Miss Gwen Gaster was one of those rare personalities who was completely at one with her purpose in life. She looked after the older children and mothered the new babies. She never learned the language properly and yet she ran everything smoothly, and somehow managed to get whatever she wanted for her babies, no matter from what source.

After the war Pastor Christoffel, now an old man, returned to the country. Miss Gaster willingly handed back the boys' section of the work, while continuing to look after the girls' school under the responsibility of the diocese, in an institute called Nur Ayin, the Way of Light.

Later on, when Pastor Christoffel died, the boys' work was moved to a larger site in Isfahan and enlarged, under the new leadership of Herr Weisinger in Germany, to become the Christoffel Blindenmission, now one of the biggest missions of its kind in the world, operating in many countries. After a few years they integrated their activities with the diocese. So once again we came to be responsible for two centres, now much bigger than before, Nur Ayin Institute for the girls, and the Christoffel Organization for the Blind, for the boys.

During the land reforms which took place under the Shah in the 1960s, a landowner, a friend of the diocese, granted us a plot of land outside Isfahan. At the suggestion of the World Council of Churches' Inter-Church Aid, we turned the land into a farm to which blind men came from all over the country to be trained in agriculture and afterwards to be rehabilitated in their villages. The project was efficiently run by the Algemeen Diakonaal Bureau of the Reformed Church of Holland, and was a striking piece of Christian service and witness. So far as I know there was nothing like it in the whole of the Middle East.

So, by the time of the Revolution, after over a hundred

years of missionary endeavour, the work for which the diocese was responsible looked like this:

Churches established in six main towns;
Eight clergy: five Iranians and three expatriates;
Two hospitals in two main towns with both expatriate and national staff;
Two clinics: one in a small village outside Isfahan and one in the town of Yazd;
The Christoffel Centre for the Blind;
The Nur Ayin Institute for the Blind;
The Cyrus the Great Training Farm for the Blind;
Schools and hostels for boys and girls.

Altogether there were thirty to forty expatriates working in these institutions. The total membership of the church was about 4,000, of whom half were expatriates from English-speaking countries, including workers in the oilfields. During a hundred years the Anglican Church had baptized altogether about 3,000 men, women, and children.

Were we justified, being so small, in spreading our activities so widely?

First of all, it must be emphasized that we had never acquired property for the sake of property itself. Most of it we had inherited from the CMS and other missions such as the Christoffel Organization. We regarded our institutions as our way of serving the community in which we lived. Our hospitals were much needed, and they were always full. People clamoured to enrol their children in our schools. Until the government, and later certain Muslim groups, started their own blind institutes, our blind work was the only facility of its kind. These institutions were our contact with the ordinary people of the country. They were the expression of the presence of Christ amid Islam. Besides, they were our identity. Without them it would be very difficult for us to exist as a visible Christian presence of mainly convert members in a Muslim society.

Another factor complicated matters even more: that without the help of foreign missionaries, our establishments could not have been run as 'Christian institutions'. Other Protestant missions in the past had simplified the position by keeping their big institutions under the control of their Home Boards, so that there existed a clear distinction between what belonged to the indigenous church and what to 'foreign missions'. The Anglican concept of the Church does not allow this. The Church of Christ is his Body on earth, and wherever it is it must be seen to be supranational and above race or colour.

There was a time, when I was about eighteen years old and thinking of offering myself for ordination, when the involvement of the local church with expatriates had worried me a great deal. I felt the weight of criticism from my fellow-countrymen who suspected Iranian Christians of allying themselves with foreigners. I remember discussing it with Bishop Thompson, who was sympathetic, but logical.

'If you really have a call from God to go and work separately for Christ like a dervish,' he told me, 'of course you are free to do so. But what will you do when you start making converts? Will you start a new church on your own, or will you join with the church that already exists?'

I saw then that the first kind of church would not really be part of the Body of Christ because it would be an isolated, exclusive, national body. The second option involved problems, but was the only true way to follow. I realized that the concept of a multi-national and multi-racial Christian community was too precious to be sacrificed, and I have upheld the idea ever since. I knew that one day we might have to pay heavily for this, and indeed we have done so; but is it possible to achieve anything sublime without sacrifice?

Our church, because it had been started by British missionaries, and because our hospitals and schools had

31

been run by them, was naturally branded as something 'British': the supremacy of the British influence in the country until after the second world war had further contributed to this. I therefore deliberately made a point of welcoming missionaries from Germany, Holland, and the United States of America. At the same time we aimed to strengthen the indigenous character of the church. The number of clergy rose at one time to twelve: six Iranians and six expatriates. Among the six Iranians, three of them had Muslim backgrounds and three came from the minority religious groups within the country.

So in the Episcopal Church community of Iran we had all kinds of races and nationalities living happily together. There were converts from Judaism, from Islam, and from Zoroastrianism living side by side and enjoying membership in the Body of Christ with their brothers and sisters from Britain, America, India, Pakistan, Germany, and Holland—an example of a healthy multiracial society on earth.

In the year 1971, when the whole country lavishly celebrated the 2,500th anniversary of the monarchy in Iran, the churches were invited to hold a joint service of thanksgiving. This was the only such ecumenical event ever to take place in Iran. Armenians, Assyrians, the Church of the East, Roman Catholics, Protestants, and Anglicans took part; I preached in Persian while the rest of the service was conducted in Armenian, Assyrian, and English. There was a mixed congregation of Christians and Muslims, ordinary citizens and officials. It was an occasion for our Persian-speaking church to be officially recognized as one of the churches of the country. It was perhaps significant that the Armenians would not allow the sermon to be preached in the Persian language in their church building, so one of the Roman Catholic churches acted as host to us.

The heads of the religious minorities were invited to attend the main celebrations at Persepolis—all that is, except me. However, this must have been an oversight on somebody's part, since the day before the ceremonies I received an urgent telephone call at our Tehran office telling me that an invitation was on the way and I must get ready to travel. I just managed to get there in time.

At the end of the celebrations we were given an audience with the Shah in one of his palaces. This was the first time I had had a chance actually to converse with him. Of course, I had seen him many a time. The first occasion was when I was on military service during the war. About seventy of us had just been commissioned as officers in the Iranian army at a simple ceremony at the famous Gulistan Palace. Among the seventy had been Mr Hoveida, who later on became Prime Minister and who was shot by the revolutionaries, and Mr Muhsen Khajeh Nouri, who was shot at the same time.

Whenever the Shah came to Isfahan, we were asked to go to stand at the airport to greet him as he passed by. But that day in his palace at Sa'adabad I actually sat next to him, with about thirty other religious leaders, mostly from other countries.

He asked me whether I was an Iranian. I told him that I was from Isfahan, and reminded him of the visit he and the Empress Farah had paid to our hospital and blind school with Queen Elizabeth during her state visit in 1961, the last year that Bishop Thompson was bishop. My impression of the Shah was of a man of piercing intelligence, anxious to make an impression, especially on expatriates, but not endowed with the rare gifts of humility and wisdom, which after all are very much interrelated.

Throughout the 1970s, as the Shah's regime grew ever more dictatorial and oppressive, we knew that we, like other organizations, were being closely watched by the secret police. We were often conscious of their presence in our church services. Every now and then they would telephone me to ask questions. Sometimes I was asked for the text of my sermons. Once I mentioned that one of the followers of Jesus was a revolutionary. A few hours afterwards, they telephoned to ask me where I had got this information!

Surveillance had been going on for a long time, of course, and from extreme Muslim groups as well as the SAVAK. As far back as during the war the Interchurch Literature Committee of Iran, a joint effort by the Presbyterian Church and the Anglicans in producing and distributing Christian literature, had started a high-quality monthly magazine, *Nur-e-Alam* ('Light of the World') under the editorship of a very able young convert from Islam. After a few years pressure was brought to bear by the police in Tehran to stop its publication. When the two churches protested and asked why their publication was banned, they were told that 'Qum was uneasy about it'. Qum is the stronghold of Shi'ite Islam in Iran.

Very soon after the war we had noticed an increase in local opposition to our evangelistic activities, both in church buildings and in private homes. Young people came in to upset the meetings in any way they could. When that was brought under control, they adopted another tactic. Groups of twos and threes would stand outside the gates of our churches to see who was attending our services. Sometimes they would send someone disguised as an 'enquirer' in order to spy on the real enquirers.

As time went by they became more organized, and expanded their activities to cover all our churches throughout the country. Several times they smashed the windows outside our buildings where Bible verses and religious pictures were displayed. They frequently threatened church members and prevented them from coming to church.

We knew that some of these young people belonged to a group called the *Anjuman-e Tablighat-e Islami*, the Islamic Propaganda Society, whose headquarters were apparently in Qum, since from time to time I would receive religious literature from there, both in Persian and in English. I was prepared to respect their religious zeal, and I expected that they would also respect our right to spread our own religious message.

However, as time went on these groups became more and more aggressive, so much so that we began to suspect their genuineness. Surely the SAVAK would not allow young people to harass minorities so openly? So we developed a theory that the SAVAK had infiltrated them with their own men, to spy both on them and on us. This theory was strengthened by the fact that, when we complained to the regular police, there seemed to be no results.

By the late 1970s oppression was universal in the country. There was no longer any doubt that we were living in a police state. The whole country was demanding freedom, and the church added its voice to those who condemned oppression.

When the Revolution came, we welcomed it. But it was not long before we found that we had exchanged one form of oppression for another even more severe.

4
Suddenly a Whirlwind

'When the day came that Job's sons and daughters were eating and drinking in the eldest brother's house, a messenger came running to Job and said, "The oxen were ploughing and the asses were grazing near them, when the Sabaeans swooped down and carried them off, after putting the herdsmen to the sword; and I am the only one to escape and tell the tale." While he was still speaking, another messenger arrived and said, "God's fire flashed from heaven. It struck the sheep and the shepherds and burnt them up; and I am the only one to escape and tell the tale." While he was still speaking, another arrived and said, "The Chaldaeans, three bands of them, have made a raid on the camels and carried them off, after putting the drivers to the sword; and I am the only one to escape and tell the tale." While this man was speaking, yet another arrived and said, "Your sons and daughters were eating and drinking in the eldest brother's house, when suddenly a whirlwind swept across from the desert and struck the four corners of the house, and it fell on the young people and killed them; and I am the only one to escape and tell the tale." At this Job stood up and rent his cloak; then he shaved his head and fell prostrate on the ground, saying:

> Naked I came from the womb,
> naked I shall return whence I came.
> The Lord gives and the Lord takes away;
> blessed be the name of the Lord.'
> (Job 1.13–21)

The Book of Job in the Bible has always been a favourite of mine. Back in 1948, when as a theological student I had been beset by doubts and had come near to losing

36

my faith, it was that book which helped me finally to stop questioning God and place my whole trust in him as Father. Now, thirty years later, it was again to become very real to me as our Church was called to go through experiences not dissimilar to those recorded by the ancient biblical writer.

In the late afternoon of Monday 19 February 1979 I was sitting alone in the small room behind my study where I go when I want to be quiet, when I was disturbed by a knock on the door.

It was John McDouall, with Dr Ronald Pont, the medical superintendent of our Isfahan hospital.

'There has been a phone call from Shiraz,' John told me. 'They tried to ring you but they couldn't get through. Arastoo is dead.'

I was stunned. Arastoo Syah was our senior priest and a valued colleague. 'How. . . ?' I managed to ask.

'It looks like he was murdered,' John said. 'Kamran found him a short while ago.'

It appeared that late that morning Arastoo Syah had been seen entering the church office, which stood a little way from the other buildings on the compound, accompanied by two enquirers whom he knew well, and whom he had been counselling for some time. He and his family had been invited to lunch with friends, and by one o'clock, as he had not arrived, they started the meal without him, assuming he had been called away on urgent business. It was not until about three o'clock that his eldest son entered the office to find his father's severely mutilated body lying in a corner.

My thoughts flew at once to the widow and two sons, and to the bereft congregation at Shiraz. I would have to break the news to his sister, who lived in Isfahan, and then set about organizing the journey to Shiraz, about 380 miles away to the south, for the funeral.

We left the next morning and arrived in time to call on the local Ayatollah in the afternoon. The Ayatollah received us kindly, expressing his profound sorrow and regret at the crime, which he said was the work of anti-revolutionaries, a term which was becoming increasingly fashionable. The police, who had been completely disorganized since the start of the Revolution, professed ignorance of the identity of the assassins. The two men with whom Arastoo had last been seen called openly on his widow the following day with a bouquet of flowers, and though they were closely questioned by the police, they were not held as suspects.

Arastoo had been very much respected in the local community, and the funeral service was a wonderful witness to the hope we have in Christ for the future—as it always is in a non-Christian environment. I had a long talk with his family, who decided shortly afterwards to leave Iran and go to live in Britain. Hasty arrangements had to be made for lay members of the congregation to take on responsibility for the church, and for clergy from other towns to visit Shiraz for the celebration of Holy Communion once a month.

I was obliged to return to Isfahan almost immediately for a conference of all the clergy, which had been arranged for three days later. During this conference, the British doctor, John Coleman, who had recently joined us at my invitation to run the clinic in Yazd, was to be ordained deacon. The quiet day preceding the ordination service was a solemn occasion as we faced together the possibilities for the future. It was obvious that difficult days lay ahead for all of us; for some it could even mean martyrdom. I told the small group of clergy that each was free to leave the country if, after prayerful consideration, he felt he should do so. My wife and I had already decided we must stay. When we met again in the evening, all of them said that they were prepared to remain. So we prayed together and committed our diocese to God before separating to our various places of work, knowing that we faced a sombre future.

Within the next few months two of the expatriate

clergy had to leave—one for family reasons and the other, who was a chaplain to the Americans and Europeans working in the oilfields, was sent home when they all left the country. Some time later one of the remaining Iranian clergy resigned to join his Australian wife who had already gone back to her home country with their three children.

During the second week of the Revolution a group of men turned up at our hospital in Isfahan, claiming to be members of the 'Revolutionary Committee' and demanding that all evangelistic activity should cease forthwith. They confiscated all our stocks of Christian literature and padlocked and sealed the room where they were kept. Later, three of them returned and announced that they had been assigned by the Committee to supervise the administration of the hospital, and forced Dr Pont to put a room at their disposal.

Contrary to the impression given by the news media at the time, this was in no sense an official government take-over, nor an attempt by the State to nationalize the privately-run hospital. The men who occupied the hospital were self-appointed and had no right whatsoever to interfere with our work. All were well known to us. They were members of the *Anjuman-e Tablighat-e Islami*, the Islamic Propaganda Society, who for the past twenty years had been in the habit of standing outside the church gate, distributing anti-Christian literature and threatening our members. None of them had any knowledge of medicine or of hospital administration, and their motives were purely political. One of their first 'reforms' was to stop the hospital buying milk from a Jewish woman who had been supplying it for more than twenty years, on the grounds that she was a non-Muslim. It soon became clear that their real purpose was to organize an opposition group against us within the hospital. It took them about three months to do this, during which time the atmosphere became

39

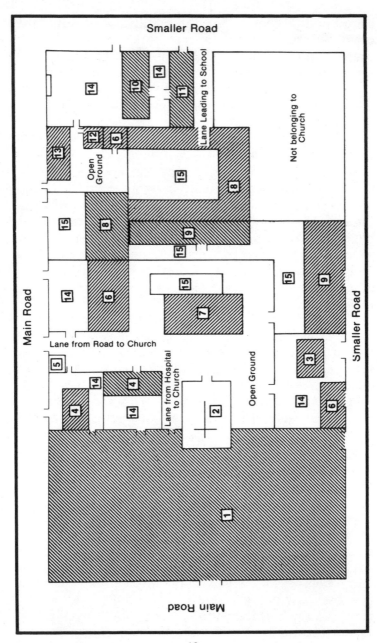

steadily more tense, particularly for the missionary staff. Discipline, which is essential for any hospital, became increasingly more difficult to maintain. Finally, on 11 June, they staged a strike and demanded that all the foreign staff should leave.

It seemed we were powerless to get any redress against this illegal action. Central government was ineffective at the time. Since the Shah had left the country, the procedure for turning a monarchical system of government into an Islamic republic was under way. Mr Bazargan, a keen Muslim, had been appointed by Ayatollah Khomainy as Prime Minister to form a provisional government. However, the system of administering the country was still basically the same. Normally, strikes would have been referred to a commission appointed by the Ministry of Labour which would seek to resolve the situation. We appealed for such a commission, but nobody seemed interested in our appeal.

I received a summons to the office of the Provincial Governor-General, along with Dr Pont and John McDouall, who was chairman of the Church's Trust Association and responsible for all our properties. Also present at the meeting were the self-appointed members of the so-called 'Revolutionary Committee' and the newly appointed head of the provincial Health Depart-

CHURCH BUILDINGS AND COMPOUND AT ISFAHAN

Key:
1 Hospital
2 Church
3 Vicarage
4 Doctors' houses
5 Doorkeeper
6 Missionary staff living quarters
7 Church hall
8 School (now rented to Government)
9 Nur Ayin Blind School
10 Bishop's house
11 Diocesan offices
12 Bishop Thompson Memorial Chapel
13 Church guest rooms
14 Gardens
15 Playgrounds

ment. Pressure was put on us to agree that the hospital should be run by a Commission appointed by the Committee with one or two representatives from among ourselves. This was an indirect way of getting us to acknowledge the authority of the Committee. Clearly it was impossible. It was also impractical. No conscientious doctor or nurse could work under a group of fanatics who had absolutely no notion of administering a hospital. The end result was that the expatriate staff left one by one, and the hospital was left in the hands of the fanatics.

I was determined not to give up the fight. John McDouall and I consulted an Isfahan lawyer, himself the grandson of a famous Ayatollah. His attitude was very clear. The action taken by the Revolutionary Committee with the help of the Governor General and the head of the Health Department was completely against all civil and Islamic laws. Although it might prove dangerous, it was my duty to stand up for the rights of the church. He drafted a short but strongly worded letter of protest which I signed and sent to Ayatollah Khomainy, Mr Bazargan, the Prosecutor General, the Minister of Justice, the Minister of Health, and the Minister of Labour. Rebukes were duly administered from Tehran to the Revolutionary Committee, but they had no effect. The fanatics would listen to nobody. Half of the hospital property was registered in the name of the Church Missionary Society and was therefore regarded as 'British property'. The newly-appointed British Ambassador, Sir John Graham, therefore sent a note of protest to the Foreign Ministry, with no practical result.

Almost exactly a month after the usurpation of the hospital in Isfahan our Shiraz hospital met with the same fate. On 12 July a group of Muslim fanatics turned out the medical superintendant, an Iranian Christian named Dr Azali, and brought in several doctors from

42

the town. The Shiraz Christian Hospital, which had been started in 1922, stood on land donated and endowed for the purpose by one of the wealthy families of Shiraz. The Endowment Document gives the responsibility of the deed to the head of the Christian Hospital. Under Islamic law 'endowment land' (*waqf*) is regarded as almost holy, and it must not be interfered with. Indeed, one of the grievances of the Khomainy movement against the Shah was that he had tampered with endowment lands. So when the militants, in the name of Islam, took by force the endowment land and all the buildings on it, we protested strongly to all the authorities.

The church building in Shiraz is adjacent to the hospital, but its grounds are registered in the name of the church. A short while after taking over the hospital the trespassers occupied the staff quarters which had been put up on the church land, and built a wall across the land haphazardly, ignoring all our protestations.

All this was a further blow to the small Christian community in Shiraz, who after the savage assassination of their pastor had not lost heart but had rather grown stronger. They still met for regular weekly worship in defiance of the fanatics, and were looking forward to welcoming one of the three remaining Iranian pastors when news came indirectly that he had left the country. His leaving at that time, without informing me directly, was a severe blow to the morale of the church.

Besides taking over our hospital properties the Revolutionary Committees had gained access to all the money in the hospitals' bank accounts. The policy of the diocese as regards our many institutions has always been that all the accounts are opened in the name of the bishop of the time, whoever he may be. He then appoints three responsible persons for each account, and every cheque must be signed by two of the three people named. Whenever they took over one of our institutions, the militants went to the bank and demanded access to the account, which to our surprise and annoyance the bank

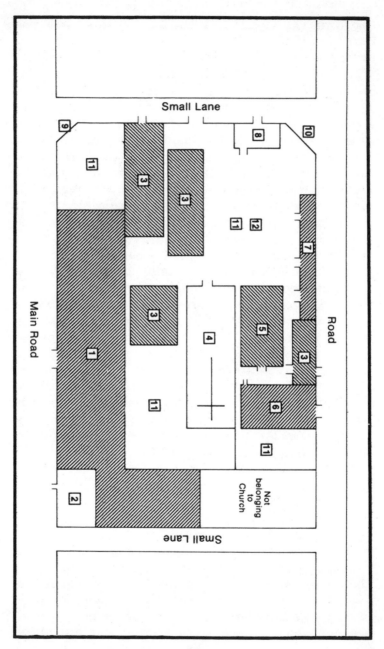

Small Lane

Main Road

Road

Small Lane

Not belonging to Church

44

managers allowed. When I took the matter up with the bank's headquarters in Tehran, the General Manager merely told me that of course I was right, and the branch managers' actions illegal, but what could they do when faced with a gun?

Apart from the separate current accounts, there was a central Diocesan Trust Fund. This had been set up by experts and was looked after by a Board of Trustees unconnected with the Diocesan Finance Committee, and was regularly audited like all our accounts. This Trust Fund money was the financial backbone of the diocese. It had grown to a very large sum, and contained among other things money for severance pay and pensions for about 200 employees who had worked in our institutions for the past forty years. The auditors had seen to it that no institution should keep much cash in its current account, and that everything beyond a certain sum was added to the Trust Fund. Our Shiraz hospital had more than others, because its administration was saving enthusiastically to rebuild the hospital.

When the revolutionaries took over the Shiraz hospital and its current accounts and went through the files, they discovered the existence of the Diocesan Trust Fund. Failing to get access to the money directly from the bank, they came to me and demanded that I hand it over to them. My answer was simple. They had acted unjustly and illegally by taking a *waqf* property by force. They had trespassed on church property. Now they

CHURCH BUILDINGS AND COMPOUND AT SHIRAZ

Key:
1 Hospital
2 Doctor's house
3 Staff houses and flats
4 Church
5 Church hall
6 Vicarage
7 Church rooms
8 Church office
9 Hospital gate
10 Church gate
11 Gardens
12 Playgrounds

were asking for money which did not belong to them. They were nothing but greedy usurpers. Besides, I was not in a position to hand over to anyone Trust money which legally belonged to the diocese.

The matter has continued to drag on, with increasingly serious consequences, until the present time.

In the second week of August 1979 the Isfahan group of revolutionaries made a further move against a Christian institution, this time the Christoffel Organization for the Blind. On the 12th, a Sunday, they invaded the compound, summarily turning out the Christian workers and their families. In charge at the time was Pastor Gerhard Lund, who was supported by the Christoffel Blindenmission in Bensheim, Germany. He lived on the compound with his wife and three young children. Also living there at the time and assisting Pastor Lund was our Diocesan Administrator, Dimitri Bellos. Dimitri is the son of a Greek orthodox father and a Russian *émigrée* mother who both became Iranian citizens. He graduated in agriculture from Shiraz University and joined the staff of the diocese mainly to administer the training farm for the blind. Later he became responsible for the administration of the whole diocese. Dimitri had married a Dutch girl, Joka, and they had two young children. Besides these two families a young Dutchman, Jan van Ingelen, was also helping with the work.

All these people were thrown out of the compound and prevented from taking any of their personal possessions. It was not until two months later that their property was finally handed over to Dimitri. By this time the Bellos family and Jan van Ingelen had moved into the house formerly occupied by the missionary nursing sisters, while the Lunds had stayed with us at Bishop's House for two weeks until they left for Germany, still without their belongings, which had to be forwarded on to them when they had been recovered.

Perhaps something should be said at this point to

explain why such blatantly lawless acts could continue to take place, apparently condoned, or at least unpunished, by the government authorities.

In the early days of the Revolution, as I have said, the system of the day-to-day running of the government remained relatively unchanged. Dr Bazargan appeared to be a democratic Prime Minister, anxious to build up the army and to strengthen the police and the law courts. Unfortunately, he did not seem to have enough power to carry out his policies. As time went on, alternative sources of authority began to establish themselves. The fanatics, who had grouped themselves into the so-called 'Revolutionary Committees' were well armed with the weapons they had looted from the army barracks, and seemed to be a law unto themselves. Apart from these, a separate phenomenon appeared under the name of the *Passdarn-e Inqelab*, the 'Guardians of the Revolution' or Revolutionary Guards, who seemed to wield more power than the army itself, and could apparently do anything they liked. They would force their way into a house, arrest anybody at will and confiscate property. Dr Bazargan often rebuked them for doing these things. Even Ayatollah Khomainy repeatedly appealed to them over the radio and television. But their lawless acts continued.

Then we began to hear of Revolutionary Courts being set up, and later young unknown mullahs appeared as 'religious judges' (*Hakim-e Shar'a*). At first there was complete confusion as to the extent of their power compared to that of the ordinary civil courts. Later on, some kind of official distinction was made. Acts against the Revolution and certain other offences such as drug trafficking came within the jurisdiction of the Revolutionary Courts; otherwise the civil courts were supposed to carry on as usual.

This explains why from the beginning the revolutionaries stigmatized the diocese as co-operating with spies active in anti-revolutionary activities, in order to be able to justify their own illegal acts as lawful, and to deal with our affairs in the Revolutionary Courts rather than the normal civil courts. It also accounts for the fact that when, for example, we continued to protest to the banks, they would write to say that they had handed over our money on the orders of the 'Revolutionary Committees' or the 'Revolutionary Courts'.

Towards the end of August I paid a visit to Yazd and Kerman, and while I was in Kerman a telephone message came through to say that fanatics had raided our Tehran premises. Our property in Tehran consisted of a guest house, a school that had been closed and was being prepared as future diocesan offices, and an unfinished church building.

The organist of the English-speaking church was staying at the guest house at the time. He was an engineer who worked for the Civil Aviation Authority of the Iranian government, and among his work papers were maps of the different airports. These were seized upon by the revolutionaries, who scattered them around in different rooms, including my study, and then declared that they had uncovered a nest of spies. Since the engineer was a British subject, Sir John Graham intervened and explained the situation to the Foreign Ministry.

It is amazing how one can become used to a succession of disasters. We took each new blow philosophically, registered a strong protest to the authorities, and wondered what would happen next. As we were adjusting to the situation and recovering from the latest shocks, an attack came on a personal level.

It was a hot summer afternoon, 29 August. My wife and I had just risen from our siesta when about thirty men burst into the house and proceeded to ransack the rooms. For all their ruffianly appearance they were obviously highly organized.

48

To my indignant challenge, 'Who are you and what do you want?' they refused to answer. I moved towards the telephone, but they had forestalled me.

Helpless, we had to watch as they systematically worked their way through the house. It was as if they were under orders to search everywhere, and to observe the layout of the house, where we slept, where we ate, where we worked. All the while they added to a pile of books and papers they were making to take away. After they had gone, we checked to find what was missing. Among other things they had taken all our family photograph albums, a list of names of all those I had confirmed since I had become bishop, the names and addresses of those who received my monthly pastoral letters, the file copies of these monthly letters for the past thirty years, and some family letters including all those our daughter Sussanne had written to us from England during the past three years.

Some of the men made their way into the diocesan offices behind the house, and brought out stacks of files which they burned on a bonfire. One of them rushed up to me in fury, brandishing a dirty, torn picture of the Shah which he had found in a pile of waste paper in Jean Waddell's office. He was dancing with rage, as if he had discovered evidence of a most heinous crime.

Jean Waddell, a Scot and a member of the Church Missionary Society, had come to work for me in January 1977. Previously she had been secretary to the Anglican Archbishop in Jerusalem. Then when the Episcopal Church in Jerusalem and the Middle East was officially inaugurated as an independent church within the Anglican Communion and I was elected as the first President Bishop, I asked that she should come to Isfahan to help me. In her fifties, she found learning a new language somewhat difficult, but her knowledge of the area and her love for the Church were a very great help to me, to the diocese, and to the Church as a whole.

When every office in Iran had a picture of the Shah

on the wall, someone had put one up in Jean's office. Later, on the fall of the Shah, the office keeper had taken the picture down and left it among a pile of unwanted papers.

Eventually the raiders left, clutching their looted papers with the air of a victorious army having sacked an enemy fortress. The moment they were out of the house, I telephoned a number I had been given only the day before by someone who had introduced himself as a Revolutionary Guard. The polite voice at the other end of the line expressed surprise and regret and very much wanted to know who the raiders were. We had recognized one of the men, and gave his name.

Looking back at the event, I would not put it beyond the bounds of possibility that I was actually talking to a member of the same group which had organized the raid. Anyway, no action was taken. We also informed the police, but they seemed even less competent than the Revolutionary Guards. A further protest to central government yielded no results.

Following the raid, our young Dutch colleague Jan van Ingelen, who was a mechanic, fixed up an ingenious alarm system with switches at various points about the house which, if pressed, would set the bell ringing in the Bishop Thompson Memorial Chapel. Privately, I thought that the steady tolling would be unlikely to alarm any raiders, but it might summon help from those who knew the signal.

About two weeks after the raid, we received an anonymous message: 'We looted your house, we tried to frighten you, but you have not gone away. We shall be back!'

5

From the Gates of Death

For almost a month we were left in comparative peace. Then suddenly, things began to happen, so swiftly and with such complexity that they had better be told in order of the dates on which they took place.

1 October 1979

I had just finished preparing the agenda and programme for the forthcoming meeting of the Diocesan Council (the last for the time being, as it turned out), when unexpected visitors arrived: one of the sons of Dr Azali, with the doctor's sister and her husband (these last two were not Christians). Dr Azali was the medical superintendent of our Shiraz hospital, who had been arrested and held prisoner by the revolutionaries. He somehow believed that if the diocese would agree to pay over the Trust Fund money, he would be released. It was impossible to be sure if this was in fact so; those who knew the Shiraz situation well were convinced that it was not. I explained yet again that I was powerless to hand over the money, but agreed to discuss the matter with the diocesan Finance Committee when it met in two days' time.

3 October

News reached me that the revolutionaries had occupied the Training Farm for the Blind outside Isfahan. The Algemeen Diakonaal Bureau of Holland, who had supported this project had found it increasingly expensive, and they had already told us they would not be able to continue. The diocese was in the process of trying to find other sources of support when it was forcibly taken over.

3–6 October

The Diocesan Council Meetings. We had much to discuss. The Council agreed with me that it would not be legal for us to part with the Trust money.

On 5 October Dr John Coleman was ordained priest. This brought the number of clergy to four, besides myself: two Iranians and two expatriates.

Iraj Muttaheddeh, the senior of the Iranian priests, had first begun attending our church services in Isfahan as a student in 1948. Jewish by birth, he was a quiet, shy, scholarly young man. Eventually he was baptized and confirmed, and later he offered himself for ordination and was sent for training to the United Theological College in Bangalore, India. After his ordination he had served as a priest in Shiraz and Tehran, and was now at Isfahan, where I asked him to remain. He is married to a Jewess, a second generation Christian, and they have three children. Iraj is a thinker. His sermons and his writings have great depth. He has translated a devotional book, *Seven Steps to Heaven*, into Persian.

Nussratollah Sharifian comes from a very different background. He is a tribal man from southern Iran, and was attracted to Christianity when he was a labour ringleader in a factory in Isfahan during the restless times after the second world war. Nusratollah was eventually baptized and confirmed, and for some time he worked in one of our bookshops. He married one of his relations, and due to certain difficulties he resigned from his employment with the diocese. For some years after that he worked for Point IV Plan, an American organization then working in Iran and other Third World countries. But Nussratollah was restless. He always wanted to serve the church. Finally he asked to be accepted as a candidate for ordination, and he too went to Bangalore with his wife for training. He was pastor in charge of the church at Kerman.

Paul Hunt, a CMS missionary, had come to Iran in 1974 to act as my chaplain and serve as pastor to the expatriate community in Isfahan. I now had to ask him and his wife Diana to move to Tehran, where Paul would take responsibility for both the English-speaking and the Persian congregations.

Dr John Coleman knew Iran well, having first come out as a CMS missionary with his wife Audrey in 1948. For sixteen years he was medical superintendent of the hospital in Shiraz, where he was very much loved and respected. Then they had to return home for the education of their children. When in the 1970s the diocese decided to open a clinic in the desert town of Yazd, some 200 miles south of Isfahan, I invited John to take charge of it, and he and Audrey returned to Iran at the end of 1977. The clinic, which was a joint effort between the town of Yazd and the diocese, was officially opened at a simple ceremony on 1 June 1978 with representatives of both town and diocese present. It was doing a fine service to the poor of the town and the villages round about. John loved the work and went round the villages twice a week. His ordination provided a much-needed addition to our small staff of priests, and he would be responsible for two congregations, in Yazd and Shiraz about 300 miles away across the mountains, in addition to his medical work.

So the pastoral care of the church in the whole of the country now rested on these four ordained men.

I formally notified the Council that I had to be away from the country for about six weeks from the beginning of November. As President Bishop of the Church in Jerusalem and the Middle East, I had certain duties outside my own diocese, and there were meetings to attend in Cyprus, in England, and in Mombasa, Kenya. I appointed Iraj Muttaheddeh as my senior commissary and Nussratollah Sharifian as junior commissary. They would look after the affairs of the diocese in my absence, together with Dimitri Bellos as Diocesan Administrator and the respective committees. I thank God for the faithfulness with which they carried out their duties for as long as they were able.

6 October

Dr Azali telephoned from Shiraz, saying that the revolutionaries had set him free, which I was delighted to hear. But, he said, they had released him on the pledge that he would persuade me to hand over the money, and he was to tell me that if I did not do so, they would arrest me. I replied that I could not prevent them arresting me, but that I could not hand over the Trust's assets.

7 October

We were entertaining guests in the evening, when Dr Azali arrived with two other men, one of them a Mr K., who had once worked as a telephonist at the Shiraz hospital, but had been dismissed for being unreliable. He had made a friend of Pastor Syah, who at his request had instructed him in the Christian faith and eventually baptized him. Since then he had been working as a clerk, and for some time lived rent free in rooms on church premises in Bushire. When the Revolution started, we found him to be a member of the local Revolutionary Committee, and when challenged about his Christian faith by church members he claimed that he had never been a Christian but had infiltrated the church to spy on the Christians.

The three men continued to pressurize me about the money, while I continued to try to convince them that it was impossible to accede to their demands. Finally they left, angry and threatening, 'We will go now, but we'll be back tomorrow, or perhaps even in the middle of the night, to arrest you!'

8 October

In the morning the men turned up again, in a van with two other young men who announced themselves as Revolutionary Guards. Also with them was Mr V., whom we had known for a long time as probably the bitterest enemy of our church. He had made himself administrator of the Isfahan Hospital, which accounted for his friendship with Mr K., who was after the same job in the Shiraz hospital.

The men asked me to come with them in the car. I knew it was an arrest. I had managed to spend over an hour in the chapel, praying and preparing myself spiritually beforehand. Now I put on my cassock, so that there should be no doubt as to my vocation. As we drove off, they told me that we would eventually be going to Shiraz; but first we were to go to the building which housed the headquarters of the Revolutionary Committee, the Revolutionary Guards, and the Revolutionary Court. It had been built some ten years ago for the SAVAK, and had not lost its sinister reputation. Everybody knew that on many occasions people had been shot here following a perfunctory 'revolutionary trial' consisting of a few questions.

As soon as we arrived I was taken into a room in front of the Revolutionary Judge, a Mr I., who did not seem to be very interested or concerned. I had the impression that nobody quite knew what to do with me. Then they took me out into the courtyard. The whole place seemed to be in a state of confusion, with young people wandering around with guns, seemingly to no purpose. I walked about for a bit, or sat on a chair which happened to be there, meditating most of the time. Fortunately I like to be by myself and to be quiet. They gave me lunch, then took me to a small room where I was locked in. K. and V. seemed to have disappeared by this time.

There was a thin blanket and a pillow on the floor of the room, which otherwise held only a metal chair; it looked very like a prison cell. The first thing I did was to draw a line on the wall with my finger nail, to count the days just in case I was going to be there for a long time.

After a while, a note came from Margaret, which cheered me very much. 'I am very proud of you for standing up for the truth,' she wrote, and asked if I needed anything. I was allowed to write back explaining that I might be taken to Shiraz, and would need some personal things for the journey. In any case, I said, I would like to have my Bible, some books, and paper and pencil.

However, after only about an hour, I was taken to yet another room upstairs. There I was asked to sign a written statement that I would notify the Revolutionary Council if I wanted to leave the country, and also that I would report to their headquarters in person whenever summoned to do so by telephone. I agreed to the first condition, but objected that I could not promise to report on the strength of a telephone call, since there would be no proof of who was calling. At last they agreed that if they wanted me they would summon me in writing. This proved to be very important.

After this, to my surprise and delight, I was told I could go. On my way through the courtyard the young revolutionaries gathered round me, asking questions about my religion. One or two of them had been to Rome, where they had seen monks and nuns and had attended church services out of curiosity. Someone wanted to know what the mass was. So, in the short time I had, I was able to tell them the story of the Cross and of the institution of the Lord's Supper.

Outside the gate, Dimitri was waiting with a car to take me home. When they had driven me away in the morning he had gone straight to the office of the Governor General Mr Bujnourdy and complained that it was a serious matter to arrest the Bishop. The Governor General had then got in touch with Tehran, who had immediately intervened and ordered me to be set free. I was most grateful to Dimitri for his prompt action, and wrote a letter of thanks to the Governor General which he answered with a kind note. I was glad to see that there was still some law and order and common sense in high places.

15–21 October

On Monday, the 15th, I had to go to Tehran for a few days on a pastoral visit, and also to obtain the necessary visas for our forthcoming trip abroad. Margaret was to go with me, and we planned to be away until just before Christmas. I had already informed the Revolutionary Committee in writing of my intention, as we had agreed.

Unexpectedly on the Saturday that week there was a telephone call, ostensibly from the Revolutionary Court, recalling me to Isfahan, a distance of about 360 miles.

'Is it that important?' I protested. 'I'm extremely busy.'

'Oh, it will only take about an hour—perhaps half an hour,' the voice assured me.

'All right, when do you want me to come?'

'You are to come today.'

'But it is Saturday today. Tomorrow I have services all day.'

'Okay, come on Monday morning. We expect you at half past ten.'

22 October

I did not manage to get home until just before noon on Monday. There was no written confirmation of the telephone call. In view of the court's undertaking in this respect, I refused to keep the appointment. Instead, I asked Dimitri Bellos to go and obtain a letter. He came back, saying he had seen the head of the court, who knew nothing about the matter, and had said that in his opinion there was no need at all for me to have come from Tehran.

Later in the day the telephone rang. An irate voice demanded to know why I had not reported. I repeated my insistence on a written invitation.

23 October

By the next morning I had the official summons, signed,

57

not by the head of the court, but by the Religious Judge—*Hujatol-Islam* Fattollah Omid-Oaemi. This was the first time I had come across this phenomenon of a Religious Judge in real life. The term occurs in old writings and is definitely a historical position, but his authority and jurisdiction have never been clearly defined. As I have explained, the whole judicial system was in a state of confusion. There were the normal civil judges, who still existed, the Revolutionary Court and its judges, and now this religious figure in turban and brown cloak. It appeared that the Religious Judges were able to pass a death sentence on anybody at any time, and they would be obeyed. I must state here that this is in no way in accordance with Islamic justice or with Shari'a law, by which to condemn a person to death there has to be a great deal of investigation, evidence, and true witnesses. Arbitrary judgements such as became prevalent during the Islamic Revolution in Iran are totally unislamic.

However, this was not the time for academic research into religious jurisprudence. I put on my cassock and Dimitri drove me to the court where he sat beside me at a table round which a few others were seated.

It appeared that this was meant to be a trial; but of course I had not been told. I had merely thought they wanted to ask one or two questions. It did not look like a trial either, but they thought it was. The Religious Judge was a youngish mullah with a gentle voice. The accusers, some of whom I recognized, were those who had usurped our institutions and stolen the money from our bank accounts. So I intended to be the accuser before the judge, and to claim redress for the crimes committed against us.

But there was no order about the court, and no opportunity to talk properly. The whole thing seemed to me rather like an unpleasant family quarrel. Every now and then someone would throw in a nasty remark, presumably addressed to me, and I would try to answer.

For instance:

'Your diocese is a nest of spies.'

'The diocese has been there for over a hundred years, serving the people of Isfahan. Have you just found out that it has been a centre for espionage?'

'Yes! We have discovered tapes and tape recorders, radio sets, and other instruments.'

'What is there in Isfahan to spy on which requires about forty expatriate workers in the fields of medicine, education, and blind welfare to spend their lives here? Is there anything about the city that foreigners do not already know? In any case, what has all this to do with me? All the expatriates have official residence and work permits. If there are spies among them, the authorities should find out, produce evidence, and deal with them. I am a bishop, not a detective.'

A change of attack:

'The Queen of England has visited your church.'

'Yes—in 1961, at the invitation of the Iranian government, and her visit was arranged by them.'

'Many foreigners come and go in your house.' (I remembered that they had taken our visitors' book!)

'Christians make no difference between a foreigner and a non-foreigner. We are all children of God, and sinners at that, and need salvation! Does not an Ayatollah meet Muslims of different nationalities?'

'The British Ambassador has been to lunch at your house.'

'As far as I am concerned, British ambassadors, or any ambassadors for that matter, are of two kinds: Christian or non-Christian. If they are Christians and attend church, I, as Bishop, have pastoral duties towards them. Sir John Graham goes to church regularly. When I was in Tehran he asked me to lunch, and when he came to Isfahan we returned his invitation. According to what law is hospitality a crime?'

'You have also had connections with the Americans. Do you know the American Ambassador?'

'When thousands of Americans live in this country and many of them come to church, of course we have connections with them. I did not know the American Ambassador, but I know Mr Bruce Laingen, the Chargé d'Affaires, because he is an Episcopalian and goes to our Tehran church. I have met him there two or three times after the service was over.'

'Your church has had dealings with the Americans in Isfahan!'

'Belhelicopter Co. rented one of our properties for their activities and we used the money for charity and church expenditure.'

I tried to bring up the question of the seizure of our properties, but to no avail. At about one o'clock the gentle-voiced judge asked me when I planned to go on my journeys. When I had told him, he brought the meeting to a close and we said goodbye, apparently in a respectful and loving manner.

This was Tuesday, and we had decided to leave Isfahan on Saturday.

26 October

In the early hours of Friday morning I heard, as if in a dream, Margaret's voice, protesting in Persian: 'What on earth are you doing here?' Then someone called me quietly: 'Bishop?'

I opened my eyes to see the barrel of a revolver less than a foot away from me. Then I heard shots—five or six of them. The noise was hollow and not very loud. Apparently this is always the case if one is very near the shot. Margaret, who had thrown herself across me, began to scream, and almost automatically I followed suit.

How swiftly the mind works! In those brief moments I remember thinking, 'Screaming is no longer any use. The thing has been done.' With a sense almost of relief I felt the load of responsibility lift from me, and like a bird I was ready to go.

The next moment I heard Margaret outside, shouting in Persian at the attackers, who were running away. I got out of bed and touched my head and neck, feeling for holes and blood, but I seemed to be unharmed. I thought perhaps the bullets might have been dummies.

Margaret came back into the room.

'What was all that about?' I asked. 'Did they come to frighten us?'

'I don't know,' she said, 'but they have got away. I followed them to make sure they had gone, because I was afraid they might come back again.'

She had chased the assailants as far as the end of the garden, about 100 yards, and had pulled down a metal fence they had used to help them climb the wall. Her left hand was streaming with blood.

'You've hurt yourself,' I said, concerned.

'No, I think one of the bullets hit it,' she replied quietly, with typical British understatement.

We looked at my pillow. There were four neat holes in a semi-circle round where my head had been, and the trace of another bullet at the head of the bed.

We rang up the police and the Revolutionary Guard and soon the house was full of people. Margaret had to be taken to the clinic where we waited an hour for a surgeon to arrive. When finally the hand was X-rayed, stitched, and set in plaster, the police escorted us home where their colleagues were still conducting their investigations.

The very efficient police major had opened up the two pillows and found four lead bullets, and another one under the bed.

'Are those real?' I asked when he showed them to me.

He looked at me in astonishment. 'Any one of these could have killed you,' he assured me.

He was unable to find a sixth bullet, neither could he be sure whether only one person had fired, or two.

There had been three men altogether. Finding all the

gates to our garden locked, they had climbed on to the roof of the diocesan offices from a narrow lane behind the buildings, by means of a lamp post, and then dropped down into the garden with the help of a convenient tree. They went to my brother's room on the ground floor and demanded where the key to the gate was kept. When he said he did not know, one of the men held a pistol to his head while the others found a piece of old iron fence which they placed up against the wall as a getaway ladder, then they forced their way into the house and came upstairs to our room.

Friends in the church were shocked and concerned when they heard what had happened, and were quick to express their sympathy. Our narrow escape had given us further cause for worry; the next day we were due to go to Tehran and then on to Cyprus, and we would be leaving Guli and Shirin behind. Naturally we were anxious about their safety. Yet at the same time we were somehow confident that the God who had saved us so miraculously would protect them also.

Later we learned that thousands of people had been praying for us: one group at almost the very time that the crime was being committed. Familiar verses from the Prayer Book version of the Psalms kept going through my mind. They might have been written especially for us:

'Thou art about my path, and about my bed.' (139.2)

'O Lord God, thou strength of my health: thou hast covered my head in the day of battle.' (140.7)

'Keep me from the snare that they have laid for me and from the traps of the wicked doers.' (141.10)

'Have mercy upon me, O Lord; consider the trouble which I suffer of them that hate me: thou that liftest me up from the gates of death.' (9.13)

On Friday 2 November Margaret and I said goodbye to our son Bahram at Mehr Abad airport in Tehran. I did not know that this would be the last time I would see him on this earth. He was a very independent young man and wanted to live his own life, and yet at this time in our country's history he wanted to be near his family. The attempt on my life had greatly shaken him, and had made him feel somehow more responsible for all of us. I shall never forget the soft touch of his newly grown beard on my face when I kissed him goodbye.

6

Torn Two Ways

Two days after leaving Tehran we heard the news of the raid on the United States Embassy and the taking of the hostages. Then came the resignation of Mr Bazargan. We knew this meant that from then onwards the fanatics would have the upper hand, and chaos would prevail.

Though I still intended to go back to Iran, I was strongly advised by almost everyone whose opinions I valued, both inside and outside the country, not to return at present. So, reluctantly, I remained in England while Margaret went back to spend Christmas with Shirin, Bahram, and Guli.

Early in the new year, Bahram telephoned from Tehran to say that he hoped to come to Europe shortly, only his passport was being withheld. He seemed optimistic that he would soon get it back.

In addition to his teaching in Damavand College at the foot of the mountains just outside Tehran, Bahram was now spending his spare time acting as translator and interpreter for the foreign newsmen who abounded in the capital. He enjoyed this extra job, which brought him into contact with all the personalities of the Revolution. Several times he accompanied reporters to Qum when they interviewed Ayatollah Khomainy and the new President, Dr Bani-Sadr. He was able to tell Dr Bani-Sadr about the problem with his passport, and the President promised to look into it.

Our daughter Sussanne was to be married on 29 March. Margaret, Shirin, and Guli flew over to England for the occasion. However, to our great disappointment, Bahram was unable to get his passport back no matter how he tried. Apparently even the President had no power over whoever was withholding it.

In Tehran they told him that the source of the trouble

was Isfahan. So he went to Isfahan where he saw the head of the Revolutionary Court, Mr I., who had interviewed me the previous October.

'We have nothing against you,' he was told. 'It's your father who is causing all the trouble.'

When asked what they had against me, Mr I. replied that the source of the trouble was Shiraz. The Revolutionary Committee were angry with me over the matter of the Trust Funds.

At this Bahram protested forcefully against the injustice of having his passport withheld because his father would not stoop to dishonesty.

'Be careful,' he was warned. 'that statement alone could be enough to get you arrested.'

So, because of man's inhumanity to man, we were deprived of the presence of our only son at our first family wedding.

Meanwhile a series of vicious attacks had started in the press and on radio and television against me personally, against my staff, and against the diocese. Extraordinary stories, more like James Bond thrillers than real life, were being published, using as evidence some of the photographs and letters which had been stolen from our house and the offices, both in Isfahan and Tehran. The text of these letters was quite harmless at the time they were written; but in the hands of the fanatics some twenty, or ten, or five years later, they were seen to be filled with imaginary plots and were quoted at length as proof that we were spies. For instance, in 1958 or thereabouts, the question had arisen of the stipend of a certain missionary priest. Bishop Thompson had proposed that the stipend should be shared equally between the Diocesan Central Budget, the CMS, and the expatriate community in Tehran where the priest was located. The bishop's letter to the leader of the expatriate community, and the written reply accepting the proposal, were among the correspondence which fell into the hands of the fanatics, and were produced as proof that the

65

diocese was receiving money from the Americans.

Arastoo Syah, who had been murdered during the first week of the Revolution, was suddenly shown to have been an agent of the Intelligence Service, assassinated by the CIA. An elderly retired Canadian clergyman, the quietest and most gentle of men, was apparently somehow involved in all this. A pretty American girl whom Bahram had known in Washington, and who had given him her picture, emerged as a most dangerous spy. Bahram was using my flat in Tehran and this photo had been among the things they had taken when they raided the premises.

Crudely-forged documents were circulated in an attempt to incriminate us. One did not need much knowledge of English to realize that they were fabrications, or that whoever had concocted them was not well acquainted with the language. They had somehow acquired letters bearing signatures of foreign Embassy officials. It was therefore a simple matter to cut out the printed insignia, paste it on to a piece of plain paper, type anything which came into their heads, and then paste underneath it the signature of an Ambassador or some other official. Photocopies, which did not show the patching-up process, were then produced as evidence.

One of these documents, purporting to be addressed to one of the CMS missionaries, and involving other missionaries and Iranian church staff, was released to the Press some time ago by the British authorities. It is reproduced in facsimile on the following page. Apart from the obvious misspellings and faulty grammar, the typing and general presentation are of a quality which no Embassy office would ever allow. Unfortunately, the so-called 'students', whose knowledge of English was scanty, were easily persuaded that such documents were genuine. Bahram, in his last telephone conversation with me, said, 'Daddy, the tragedy is that these young men really do believe what they are told by others.'

66

BRITISH EMBASSY
TEHRAN

27 Oct 1977

Miss Barbara Mitchell
St. Luke's Church
Isfahan, Iran

Dear Barbara,

Thank you for your reports, intercepted radio code messages, and
microfilms, and are pleased to inform you, we are sending   you
sensitive inteligence equipment .

On the other hand, today we sent you invisiblo inks, by separate
cover.

Don't be afraid, because Dr. Pont, Dimitri bloss, John clark,
Rev. Sharifian, Rev. Iraj Motahedeh, Rev. Paul Hunt, can assist you.
Looking forward to your early reply soon,

Yours sincerely

Tony Parsons

A D Parsons

It hurt me to know that our church members were being slandered in this way when I was not there to share the burden with them. On the other hand, my friends and colleagues continued to write urging me not to return, as my life was almost certainly at risk. Fellow bishops and archbishops who met in England after the enthronement of the new Archbishop of Canterbury on 26 March also advised me not to go back for the time being—'A live dog is better than a dead lion,' someone told me jokingly.

It was Dr John Taylor, Bishop of Winchester, a friend whose opinion I have always valued, who referred me to St Paul's words in Philippians 1.21–24: 'For me life is Christ and death gain; but what if my living on in the body may serve some good purpose? Which then am I to choose? I cannot tell. I am torn two ways: what I should like is to depart and be with Christ; that is better by far; but for your sake there is greater need for me to stay on in the body . . .' Paul would have preferred to have stayed on in Jerusalem and met his death, because that would have taken him immediately to be closer to his Lord and Master. But for the sake of the flock for whom he had been called to be shepherd, he had to choose whether to meet his death or appeal to Caesar and go to Rome, and possibly live for several more years to be of help to Christians. Had he not done this, we would not have had several of his precious letters including perhaps this one to the Philippians.

The emphasis was on the word 'choose'. I too had to choose, whether to go back to my death or to stay on and be of what use I could from a distance. If I had felt I could have been of any help at all in Iran, I would have gone back; but I was sure I wouldn't be given a chance to be of help to anyone. The reason for my certainty was my pillow case with four bullet holes in it; and no news of any arrest of those who had fired the shots.

Besides, there was still a great deal I could do outside the diocese. There was my monthly pastoral letter which needed to be kept up now more than ever, as well as personal letters to individuals in the church. There was the task of informing Christians throughout the world of the plight of the Iranian church, asking them to uphold us in their prayers. The story had to be told of all that had happened and of how we as a church had reacted. Over and above all this, there were my duties as the President Bishop of the whole Middle-Eastern Province.

Margaret and I discussed all these things. Perhaps this is the place to say a few words about Margaret, my wife. A few years after our marriage, in the 1950s, I wrote: 'Some friends who know me intimately tell me that, second to my conversion, my marriage has been the biggest miracle in my life.' Now, after nearly thirty years, I can still confirm that. There is no doubt in either of our minds that our marriage was designed by God who had called us both to serve his Church in Iran and to witness together to his love.

In every respect Margaret has been the ideal person, complementing my weaknesses in all sorts of ways. While I hesitate and analyse and wonder what to do, she gets on with jobs that need to be done, in a matter-of-fact way. If we think of the grace of God as a stream of water flowing through the field of our lives, in me the water encounters many blockages, diversions, and waste holes. Margaret's nature seems to be ready and clean for the water to run through without any difficulty or wastage. How often I have marvelled at her ability to take things as they come, never refusing to do something that needs to be done, never complaining about anything. Sometimes I have wished she would stop and analyse things before deciding, but have found that she had already done the job while I was still pulling the pros and cons of the matter to pieces; and nearly always she has proved right. While I have learned in tortuous ways to make God's vital gifts of faith, hope, and love my own, for her these gifts seem to be as natural as growth, shade, and fruit are to a healthy tree. Apparently other people also

69

have noticed these qualities in her. I was very glad when the Ross McWhirter Foundation invited her to accept their annual award for bravery and courage, and she humbly accepted it.

It did not take much discussion for Margaret to decide to go back, with Shirin and Guli, to Isfahan. Our small church community needed as much comfort as she could give them. At the same time, we became convinced that I should remain in England.

Separation was not at all easy, especially when the situation was so dangerous and the future so dark and unknown. In one of my letters to her that she has kept I wrote:

> I feel so forlorn and empty. It is far more difficult than I thought it would be; but we must bear it bravely, we cannot do it without the presence of Christ. I feel him very near and I am sure you have done too. Your faith, courage, and love for the church has been and still is a great inspiration. This separation is extremely difficult for both of us; but in spite of what people say [that she ought not to have gone back], I somehow think that we have done the right thing. We could not have let the church down, and I could not have ignored their advice [not to go back]. So you have taken the heavier burden, and therefore his grace will be all the more intense for you. Even if something awful happens and we get hurt it is worth it. After all, what is life worth, if it is not lived for a purpose higher than one's own life? And what higher purpose than to do the will of God?

I had no idea when I wrote that letter that the great hurt was going to come in a real way.

But even before the personal tragedy which struck our family we had terrible evidence that we were not the only targets for violence by the militants.

I had been invited by Bishop Leonard Ashton of Cyprus and the Gulf to take part in the joint session of

70

their Diocesan Council which was to meet in early May. At the same time he had suggested that I might make Cyprus my headquarters, and ask Jean Waddell, my secretary, who was still in Iran, to come and work for us both.

I was preparing to leave London for Larnaka when I heard the horrifying news that Jean had been shot.

Jean was in Tehran at the time, staying in a small flat she often used, next to the guest rooms on the top floor of the diocesan building. She had had trouble in obtaining permission to leave the country and had come from Isfahan to seek the help of the British Embassy.

That morning, in the flat downstairs, the Hunt family had been planning a family picnic.

'Let's go and invite Jean to join us,' suggested Diana. With her two small girls she climbed the stairs and knocked at Jean's door. There was no reply.

'She must be out,' Diana decided. 'We'll come back later.'

Little Rosemary was not so easily persuaded. 'I'm going to knock again,' she insisted, and started to bang harder.

The door burst open. Before they had time to cry out, two armed men seized the woman and children and thrust them into the bathroom of the adjoining guest flat. 'If anyone makes a noise,' they threatened, 'you will be badly hurt.'

Bravely, Diana tried to reassure the children, and for about half an hour kept them quiet until the absence of noise from the next flat suggested the men had gone. Cautiously she peered out. Finding the main flat door open, she grabbed the children and dashed down to the street to raise the alarm.

Later, Jean described the attack on herself in a tape recording which she sent to England after her recovery. The first part of it is taken from the statement she gave to the Iranian police:

71

At approximately 8.30 a.m. I opened my flat door in order to go along to the kitchen belonging to the guest rooms. As I opened the door a young gunman slipped in with his gun pointing at me. I gave a small scream just as another young man with a gun pushed his way into the room. They said they were from the Revolutionary Council. One of them spoke very good English and the other one none at all. The one who spoke English did all the talking with me. He said he wanted to ask me questions and wanted to push me into the kitchen.

I said, 'Why not come into the sitting room and put away your guns?' as I was quite happy to answer questions. They did come into the sitting room and the English-speaking young man sat down and put his gun away. The other one prowled round the flat and picked things up, showing them to the other one.

I sat down and waited for the questions. He repeated that they were from the Revolutionary Council and that the whole place was surrounded by Revolutionary Guards.

I said, 'What for? I'm a lone woman, living here on the top floor.' Then I said, 'What questions do you want to ask?'

He asked me my name and then asked if I had another name. I explained about my full name being Margaret Jean. He had my work permit in his hand when he asked me this. Then he asked me, Did I know Christopher Powell? I said, No, and that I had never heard of him. Then he asked, Did I know Paul Hunt? [Paul's full name is Christopher Paul Hunt.] I said, 'Yes of course, he is our priest.'

He asked, 'Does he live here?'

I said, 'He lives in the next flat,' and added, 'Don't go to his house as you came to mine because he has young children who would be very frightened.'

At one moment he had also asked me, 'Are you Mrs Hunt?' and I said, 'No.'

72

Then they asked me other questions.

I offered them coffee but they refused. It seemed that the whole conversation took about half an hour, then they said that I must go with them to the Revolutionary Council. I said, 'Why?'

I stood up and they said that they must blindfold me. Again I asked them why they must do this as the Revolutionary Council was not something hidden. Then he said it was the Revolutionary Guard they must take me to.

We had quite a conversation about what they should use as a blindfold and when I used a Farsi phrase the one who didn't speak English said in Farsi, 'Look, she does speak Farsi,' but I said that I only spoke it a little.

They decided to use a blouse of mine as a blindfold and one of them went behind me, but instead of blindfolding me he hooked his left arm round my neck and jerked me off my feet and the other one grabbed my feet and it seemed that they were also beating my body, also my diaphragm. It was like an explosion of violence and I felt they were trying to break my neck and cut off the air so as to choke me. I struggled to get some air. It was very painful, but fortunately I went unconscious very quickly.

Some time later—I had lost all sense of time—I woke up in my bed, bathed in sweat and thinking, 'Gosh, that was a nightmare! Thank goodness I have woken up!' Then I realized I couldn't move my feet and my hands were tied to my sides with the blouse; my feet were tied with a pair of stockings. I was very hot.

Over what seemed a long period of time I managed to free my hands and then got my feet free. I got so hot I threw the quilt off and managed to sit up, hoping to reach the desk where the 'phone was. My left side was very heavy but I didn't then realize that I had been shot. They must have shot me when I was lying unconscious.

I fell back on the bed and groaned a great deal. I do not know how long I waited. . . . My bedroom door was open, and in one of my lucid moments it was a wonderful sight to see the outside door of my flat splintered under the boots of a large Iranian policeman who simply walked through it, followed by Paul Hunt.

After that my small bedroom seemed full of people and noise, much to my delight, and I remember being put on a chair and carried out. Fortunately I don't remember the three flights of stairs, but I do remember being pushed into the ambulance to the accompaniment of many groans, and the dash to the hospital.

At the hospital, the surgeon was about to start another operation when Jean arrived. Seeing her condition, he immediately cancelled it and wheeled her straight into the already prepared theatre. His prompt action undoubtedly saved her life.

Jean was full of praise for this charming and pleasant Iranian doctor. 'His own life was threatened because he had saved mine, but I didn't hear this until much later. He just continued quietly to complete the wonderful job he had started in the operation theatre. So long as we have people like him and his colleagues there is hope for the future of Iran.'

For her attackers, she expressed nothing but pity. 'They seemed such nice living, ordinary boys, but putting all their faith in their guns. We don't know what may have happened to them in their short lives to make them do what they did to me, but on TV, almost every night, I have seen little boys and lovely girls crawling on their bellies with rifles in their hands, and going through all the drill of taking their guns to pieces and reassembling them. All this with hate and revenge in their hearts. In the midst of all this it will be a hard task for our little church to love and not to grow bitter if they suffer further blows. We must pray for them and support them in every way we can.'

As soon as Margaret heard the news about Jean she travelled by bus through the night from Isfahan, reaching the hospital about five o'clock the next morning. For a whole week she hardly left Jean's side.

'It is impossible to express just what she meant to me at that time,' Jean said. 'She seemed to breathe strength and life into me and even the touch of her hand had a special quality.'

7

Tears Ought to Freeze

I stood on a hill-top in Cyprus, on a quiet, warm afternoon in late spring. It was the site of the grave of Archbishop Makarios, high, remote, and majestic in its simplicity, rather like the Archbishop himself as I remembered him.

I remained there for some time thinking about my country and its leaders, about our tiny church and its sufferings, and about my family and what might happen to them. An extraordinary sensation of tiredness overtook me. Thoughts kept coming into my mind about our son Bahram and how he had decided to go back to Iran. I had urged him to try to get his Ph.D., but he had been adamant that he wanted to come back at once. I did not know why this thought that it was he himself who had decided to return to Iran should be so strong in me at that time in that place.

Very seldom do I walk out of meetings, but that night I felt so tired that I left in the middle of the conference session after dinner and went to my room. I looked over the notes which I had prepared for the three talks that I had to give the next day, had a bath, and went to bed.

At about 11.30 p.m. I was fast asleep when a loud knock at my door woke me. 'Telephone for you,' I heard someone say.

I jumped out of bed. 'Is it from Iran?' I called.

'No, from England,' came the answer.

I had to walk along a long corridor and down a staircase before reaching the telephone. All sorts of thoughts crossed my mind. Could it be about Jean? About the family?

When I reached the office, Bishop Ashton was speaking into the telephone.

'Bad news,' he said briefly, as he handed me the receiver.

It was Dick Ashton, Margaret's brother-in-law, speaking from London. When I had identified myself, he, too, said, 'Bad news.'

'Yes,' was all I could say.

'It's about Bahram.'

'Yes?'

'He was shot and he is dead.'

I felt quite numb. 'He will be with Paul now,' I said. Dick and Eleanor Ashton's only son, who was about Bahram's age, had recently died in tragic circumstances.

Apparently Bahram had been driving home from college early that afternoon, when two men in a car turned in front of him and forced him to stop. One of them then got into the driver's seat and forced Bahram to move across to the passenger seat, then drove on into a desert place, the other car following them. When they got near the Evin prison, they stopped. A young boy of about fourteen who happened to be passing saw the two cars and the man talking to Bahram. Then came the sound of shots and the two men drove rapidly away in the other car. The boy at once alerted the gendarmerie and they took the body to the hospital nearby. What were they talking about? We shall probably never know. It is possible that the man had a tape recorder, and wanted Bahram to testify against his father or even deny his faith. Of course Bahram would have refused.

Margaret was nursing Jean Waddell in the Tehran hospital when she heard the news. Jean said later that she was wonderful, and refused to leave her until she had found someone else to take care of her. Dick Ashton told me that the newsmen had agreed not to release the story until I had heard, which I appreciated very much. When newsmen agree to withhold their news, it shows they really care. Of course they knew Bahram, as he had been interpreting for them in all sorts of places and situations.

Bishop Ashton and his staff were extremely kind and thoughtful. They offered to make me coffee; but I wanted to be alone, so I thanked them and went to my room. I was amazed that my eyes were dry; apparently it takes some time for sorrow to heat the heart and for the steam to come out through the eyes.

My first thought was to write to Margaret:

At first I could not believe it; but soon the truth dawned . . . I immediately thought of you and wished you were next to me. It is harder to bear it alone. But I thought of Dick and Eleanor after Paul, their son's sudden and tragic death, and felt strengthened . . . I don't know what you will be doing now. May God guide and protect you, and Shirin and Guli, and bring you safely out. I feel very calm and yet bewildered. I feel I am surrounded by people praying for us. May God give us strength to bear this tragedy for his glory. Whatever I have is from God and so I am happy to give him back whatever he has kindly given . . . Of course I want to know all the details, but I realize I cannot now. I must wait . . . May God forgive the murderers of our son, because obviously they did not know what they were doing. What had he done to them? What have we done to them? He was such a good boy. He came to the country really for our sake. He was stopped from going out for our sake. He was killed for my sake. If I knew they would really kill him I would have come and would have been killed; but it never occurred to me that they really would kill him. The evil in man is far deeper than I had imagined. May God use the death of our dear son to bring about the salvation of many in a mysterious way in our country. What a good, educated, and cultured soul the country has lost! How we toiled to put him into Monkton and then how we tried to find him a scholarship at Oxford and then at George Washington. All this cannot go to waste.

Somewhere, somehow, this sacrifice will bear fruit in the economy of God: how and when and where we don't know. We must not have hatred in our hearts, only sorrow and pity for those unfortunate murderers. May God awaken their souls for them to realize the depth of sin and hatred and then be saved.

I finally fell asleep at about 2 a.m. with the help of a sleeping pill, and woke up at 6 o'clock. Bishop Ashton had suggested that I should leave the conference if I wished, or in any case take the day off, since it was my turn to lead three devotional meetings; but I thought I had better try to carry on, so I dressed and went down for breakfast. Obviously everybody had heard and the atmosphere in the hotel was full of sympathy. As people came to express their condolences my self-control gave way and the tears came streaming. I was obliged to accept my weakness and let Archdeacon Handford take the meetings instead of me. But I decided to stay in the conference, as I thought it would be better to be among friends. It certainly proved to be the right decision. Very soon everyone was taking it as naturally as possible.

Telegrams started to pour in. It was useless to try to telephone Margaret from that small village, so I decided to send a cable. Archdeacon Northridge of Nicosia was sitting beside me at breakfast and I asked him if he could think of an appropriate Bible verse. He suggested a verse from the *Daily Light* reading for that morning. So my cable included a reference to Psalm 57.1, 'In the shadow of thy wings will I make my refuge, until these calamities be overpast.'

My hobby is watercolour painting. Fortunately I had my paint-box, paper, and brushes with me, and it was a great emotional release to be able to sit and paint a view occasionally in those very tense days.

After four days the conference ended and we went back to Nicosia. The Christian community couldn't have been more thoughtful and sympathetic. Bishop

Ashton and the Northridges managed to make me feel part of the family. At the same time I was in touch with Margaret as much as possible by telephone and by letters. What I was going through was nothing compared with what she had to endure in Iran. She wanted to take the body of her son to Isfahan for burial, and this was not an easy task for a woman in the atmosphere of those days in the country. She first had to clear the formalities with the gendarmerie, the police, and the hospital; and then hire an ambulance and receive the body from Behest-e-Zahra, the cemetery which had been the focus of the Revolution and where perhaps thousands have been buried in the past two years. A university friend of mine and his family, with whom we had kept in touch over the years, were a great help to Margaret at that time. We shall always remain grateful to them.

The funeral service took place in Isfahan on 11 May. St Luke's Church was packed with people—Christians and non-Christians. Iraj Muttaheddeh took the service and preached a moving sermon. I am told the church had never been so full of flowers before. That day I wrote in my diary:

Bahram was sacrificed. God asked Abraham to sacrifice his son, but at the last moment prevented it. In our case he allowed it to happen. Bahram's was a clean sacrifice. Margaret and I shall burn in the fire of this sacrifice to the end of our lives and to the marrow of our bones. O Lord, I now understand what Mary thy mother must have gone through seeing thy body on the Cross. Your sacrifice, O Christ, saved the world, from sin, from hatred . . . O God, we see a similarity between the sacrifice of thy Son and of our son, Bahram, and through him his family have become sharers in the suffering of Christ.

The only consolation we have is this, that the sacrifice of our son may remove some of the hatred and suspicion which exist in the minds and hearts

80

of our people against the 'foreign' aspect of our church; and thus open their minds and hearts to the love of Christ; and that the church may be rooted more in the soil of our country.

O God, the only thing which keeps us sane is our faith in thy way:

The way that life comes through death.

The growth of a seed when it dies.

Resurrection after Good Friday.

O God, we as a family are going through 'Good Friday', when will the 'Resurrection' be? When will Bahram's sacrifice give fruit? But the fruits have already appeared in our hearts—the power to go on believing, hoping, and loving in spite of what has happened.

Measure thy life by loss
  and not by gain,
Not by the wine drunk, but
  by the wine poured forth,
For Love's strength standeth in
  love's sacrifice
And he who suffers most has most to give.

The day before the funeral I wrote a prayer in Persian, inspired by one written in a war-time concentration camp which had been sent to me by Sue Hargreaves, the former matron of our hospital in Isfahan. I dictated it over the telephone to be read at Bahram's funeral service. Afterwards, with the help of Bishop Ashton, I translated it into a suitable English style and we sent a copy to everyone who wrote expressing sympathy with us. It is quoted at the end of this book.

In my Persian diary there is another entry an hour and a half after what I wrote at the time of the funeral:

It is now 5 p.m. in Nicosia, which means 6.30 in Iran. By now they must have buried dear Bahram. O God, I give him into your hands. Make him have fellowship with thee. He was always keen to meet greater persons than himself. He has a good opportunity now. I wonder what effect his grave will have in Isfahan and in Iran. We are not particularly interested in the earth which is over the grave, but in what may grow out of it: the fruits of the Spirit. I wonder how much his mother and I will witness the effects of Bahram's sacrifice. Bahram dear, till we meet again in the presence of God—Goodbye!

Your Father

We had planned that Margaret, with Shirin and Guli, would fly from Tehran for London the same day that I was to leave Nicosia. Before leaving Tehran, they had two more services. One was at Damarvand College where Bahram used to teach. Most of the college attended the service, at which both Margaret and Shirin spoke, as well as some of the college staff. The other was a memorial service in St Paul's Church in Tehran, to which many of Bahram's Muslim students went and listened to a wonderfully deep and thought-provoking sermon preached by Iraj Muttaheddeh who had travelled from Isfahan for the purpose.

There is another entry in my Persian diary dated 17 May:

Although I would like to be alone and observe my sorrow, I think it is better to be with people, especially my friends, and be as natural as one can be under the circumstances. I understand that the way a microwave oven works is that the intense heat strikes at the centre of the material to be cooked, so that the food is cooked very quickly without the utensil in which the food is placed getting hot at all. I feel I am being burned from the centre of my being—the very marrow of my bones. O God, give me the strength to bear the heat of this burning. I literally feel the heat warming me up from within, bringing it to the boil and then tears flow. I wonder how his mother is taking

82

it all in Iran. How proud of her only son she was! He was the joy of her life . . . For me the nearest incident to the event of the Cross of Jesus and his sacrifice is the sacrifice of Bahram. If I did not believe in the method of God's salvation through the Cross of his son Jesus, I would not have been able to bear the sacrifice of my son . . .

I was clearly led not to go back, but the price of this was the martyrdom of Bahram. O God! If the result of the sacrifice of your Christ is that man comes to know himself and what is in him better; and then to understand the depth of your love for him, causing him to repent and come to you—what will be the result of Bahram's sacrifice? I think his mother and I have the right to ask this question . . .

This is where faith comes in! For forty years I have been speaking and preaching about the problem of suffering and its relationship with the Cross of Christ, now I have the chance of actually living through it. The fire of this suffering is roasting me, the way meat is roasted on a skewer, for the youthful life of Bahram being cut short so cruelly; but O God, you gave us Bahram, we enjoyed him for twenty-four years; now you have allowed him to come to you. You saved my life and his mother's miraculously, but not his. You accepted his sacrifice now; but you mean us to go with the sacrifice of a broken heart to the end of our lives. May men come to know of your love through these sacrifices. 'The blood of the martyrs is the seed of the Church,' so the saying goes. Will the innocent blood of Bahram strengthen the foundation of your Church in Iran? This has always been your method, is now, and ever shall be. We must have patience and complete trust in God's ways. We must bear the suffering without any hatred. Those who killed Bahram really did not know what they were doing, therefore we must pray for them from the bottom of our hearts:

Give me Thy joy, O wounded man of sorrows,
Thy joy filled full in those dark hours of pain.
Joy in Thy fellowship, despised, rejected,
Bearing all grief that Love may live again.

O God, grant Margaret, Shirin, Sussanne, Guli, and myself that same joy that you were filled with in the dark hours of your pain.

Nicosia, 17 May 1980

On 20 May I left Nicosia for London. I did not know whether or not my wife and daughters had been able to arrange their flight for the same day, but just before I boarded the plane a friend in the news world managed to find out through his contacts that they had in fact already left and would be in London about the same time as I. It was very comforting to know this.

And sure enough, there they were at London Airport, Margaret, Shirin, and Guli. Certainly tragedy brings people closer to each other. I had never felt we needed anything to make us closer; but that afternoon at Heathrow the unity we felt with each other was beyond any description. Margaret was pale and tired and the girls seemed somewhat bewildered. But we were all thankful to be together. Because of Bahram's contacts with the news media all the news and cameramen of the world seemed to be represented, and they were full of questions. It was somewhat unexpected, and we were very glad an hour or so later to be sitting at peace in the home of my wife's mother, Mrs Thompson, in London.

People were so sympathetic and thoughtful. They showed it in different ways. The Archbishop of Canterbury sent a lovely bouquet of flowers expressing his sympathy. Scotland Yard arranged for two policemen to see to the security of the house and gave me some useful advice. Some of Bahram's Oxford friends found us out and came to call. On 24 May there was a memorial service for Bahram in St Dionis' Church where Dick

Ashton is the vicar. Nearly 400 people came, and it was a glorious service of thanksgiving for Bahram's life. Bishop George Appleton, the former Archbishop in Jerusalem, who had known Bahram as a boy, preached the sermon, and Mr Robin Waterfield, who had also known him, spoke about him.

There was also a memorial service for Bahram in the Church of the Epiphany in Washington D.C., where he had spent two years at George Washington University. The Reverend Edgar D. Romig, the rector, sent us a copy of a prayer written for the occasion:

Our Heavenly Father, even as we mourn for Bahram we thank thee with deep thanks for his short but rich and loving life: for his keenness of intellect, for his love of family, and for the affectionate kindness of his spirit. We praise thee for his imagination and creativity and for the delight with which he enjoyed and added to the beauty of life in nature, in art, in music, in the theatre, and in people.

We have had over 500 letters and telegrams from all over the world, full of beautiful things about Bahram and wise words of condolence. One in particular interested and surprised us very much. We do not know how it came to us. One day it was found in Dick Ashton's letter box—an open envelope with no stamps, bearing the official insignia of the Iranian Ministry of Foreign Affairs. Our name had been handwritten on the envelope in English. It was from Mr Bruce Laingen, the U.S. Chargé d'Affaires in Tehran who had been taken hostage at the time of the storming of the Embassy and was being held in the Ministry of Foreign Affairs building in Tehran. It read:

I have been deeply shocked and saddened to read in the press a report of the tragic death of your son. No words of mortals can help at such a time, but I pray that God will give you and your family the strength and understanding that only he can provide to help at a time of

May 10, 1980
The Foreign Ministry
Tehran

Your Grace,

I have been deeply shocked and saddened to read in the press a report of the tragic death of your son. No words of mortals can help at such a time, but I pray that God will give you and your family the strength and understanding that only He can provide to help at a time of such grievous loss. I hope you will also express my concern to your Secretary, Jean Waddell, over the news of her shocking experience and my relief that she apparently is recovering.

God be with all of you,

Sincerely,
Bruce Laingen
(former Chargé d'Affaires
of the United States)

such grievous loss.

I hope you will also express my concern to your secretary Jean Waddell, on the news of her shocking experience and my relief that she apparently is recovering.

I had only met Mr Laingen two or three times, and that very briefly after divine service in St Paul's Episcopal Church in Tehran, and so was very moved to receive such a letter from him when he himself couldn't have been in happy circumstances. It spoke to us of the kind of man he must be. We wrote him a letter enclosing one of our prayers of forgiveness. Whether he ever received it, we don't know.

Another message we valued a great deal was in the form of a beautiful poem sent to us by the Welsh poet, Michael Burn:

In memory of BAHRAM DEHQANI-TAFTI
murdered in Iran, May 1980
aged 24

One winter's night, says the Cathedral booklet,
A mason hung his slate out, and it rained,
And down the slate the rain froze, perpendicular;
And in the morning the new style was born.

Tears ought to freeze into some architecture
Of words for Bahram slain. Tears ought to soar
In some west window of an ode; not shrink,
Equivocate, the Poets being embarrassed.

The Poets write, knowing he was a Christian:
'Oh yes, a brave life . . . even a beautiful . . .
Martyred for Human Rights . . .'; and that will do.
Crucifixion they can take; not Resurrection.

Not 'Faith was part of him, and those who loved him.
And God has put his faithful through the fire,
Working through suffering; but will not fail
To reunite them, and forgive his murderers.'

I never learned the language you returned to,
Or saw the country you refused to flee.
To me it just meant poverty, and domes, and princes
Sauntering through gardens among nightingales.

The East that my imagination fed on
I never dreamed would disquiet me with this death,
Or show me Oxford's happy scholar lying
Like a young saint in jewelled Isfahan.

Michael Burn

8
How Long Can This Go On?

Our friends Bishop and Mrs John Robinson, who had visited us in Isfahan, were urging us to stay in Cambridge. There was nothing we would have liked better; but first we had to be quite sure that it was the right thing for us to do. In the end, all circumstances pointed to the fact that it would not be possible for us to stay permanently anywhere in the Middle East. At the same time, a warm invitation came from the Reverend Hugo de Waal, principal of my old theological college, Ridley Hall, offering us a flat for a few months. It seemed an ideal arrangement, especially as Margaret's old school, not very far from Cambridge, offered a full scholarship to Guli for one year.

It was simply heaven to be in our own flat, and to have a study and a desk to myself after nine months of gipsy life. It was especially good to be back in Cambridge after thirty-three years, and actually living in Ridley again. So many of the links with my past life had been shattered. The buildings and institutions which formed part of my youth had long since been transformed for other purposes—my old school in Isfahan; the part of the University of Tehran I had attended. All the familiar institutions amidst which I grew up had been taken over by the militants. But Ridley is still the same, and Cambridge is the same. The 'Backs' are the same.

For the first few days I walked about like a drunken man, absorbing the intoxicating atmosphere. 'Here is my home,' I told myself. Great figures from the life of the Iranian church, names familiar to me from my childhood, were educated here. Henry Martyn, who translated the New Testament into Persian, went to St John's College. The Bridge of Sighs and the red brick building next to it have the date 1671 on the wall. 'This building,'

I thought to myself, 'was there 200 years before Henry Martyn.' Dr Donald Carr, who built the Isfahan Hospital, went to Trinity, as did Bishop Thompson, my father-in-law, who ordained me priest. While all these have gone before me, their colleges are still there and remind me of them.

But even in Cambridge we were not to enjoy peace for long. Just as we were beginning to settle down, there came the news of Jean Waddell's arrest in Isfahan. I could not believe it at first. We had heard to our great satisfaction that Jean had recovered from her bullet wound and was hoping to return to Britain, and we were looking forward to meeting her again. However, problems she had faced for some time in leaving Iran culminated in a summons to answer questions before the Revolutionary authorities in Isfahan. Accompanied by an official of the British Embassy, she travelled to Isfahan on 5 August to report to the Revolutionary Court. There she was arrested, and the Embassy official was refused permission to see her. From that day to the time of writing (November 1980), she has seen no one from the outside world, though a consular official was on one occasion permitted to send her a few books and simple necessities.

Four days later, on 9 August, three British missionaries who were running the Nur Ayin home for blind girls were summoned to the Ministry of National Guidance. They were Margaret Knill, a CMS missionary, Libby Walker, a short-service worker sponsored by CMS, and Anne White, of the Bible and Medical Missionary Fellowship. Dimitri Bellos went with them in his capacity as Diocesan Administrator. The women were given forty-eight hours to leave the country, and Dimitri was arrested there and then. No one has heard from him since. His wife Joka, who is expecting their third child, continues to help at Nur Ayin.

On the following day, John and Audrey Coleman had to go to Tehran, to the Ministry of National Guidance, to see about their residence permit. They too were immediately arrested. No reason for their detention has ever been given, and no one has heard from them or seen them since.

A week later, on 17 August, members of the Revolutionary Guard went to St Luke's vicarage in Isfahan, which stands next to the church, and arrested Iraj Muttaheddeh in the presence of his wife and three children. No one has been allowed to see him since.

Nussratollah Sharifian, my junior commissary and the pastor in charge of St Andrew's church in Kerman, was arrested on 28 August and taken to Tehran. His detention means that there is now no Anglican priest left functioning in the whole of Iran. Paul Hunt had been fortunate to be able to leave unimpeded in May.

In the meantime, allegations and slanders against our church continue over Tehran radio and television, and in the revolutionary press. Government ministers have joined in the slander. A junior official of the Department of Education in Isfahan, who was in charge of the fanatical *Tablighat-e Islami* organization in that town and is now deputy speaker of the Majlis, has publicly, and with no respect for truth, accused me and the diocese of being involved in espionage. The deputy Information Minister talks wildly about the diocese having received 500 million dollars from the CIA for distribution to officers in the army, and 300 kilogrammes of T.N.T. explosives from the British Ambassador, Sir John Graham, to be given to conspirators plotting a *coup d'état*.

No amount of denial seems to stop them from making these ridiculous and devilish allegations which have not an atom of truth behind them. The British authorities have officially denied any involvement. I have vigorously refuted the allegations in statements issued through the Anglican Consultative Council in London, calling them 'baseless, malicious lies' and denouncing the documents they claim to have as 'crude forgeries'. I have openly declared their treatment of me and my diocese as an action 'not only against the law but against Islam itself'. I have protested against the detention of church leaders and have called for their immediate release.

In September 1980 when Mr Garmarudi, the President of Iran's spokesman, visited London, I took the opportunity to write a letter to Ayatollah Khomainy, with copies to Dr Bani-Sadr, the President, and Mr Rajai, the Prime Minister. This letter, quoted in full below, I sent to Mr Ehdai, the Iranian Chargé d'Affaires in London, asking that Mr Garmarudi should deliver it on his return. I do not know if it ever reached its intended destination.

c/o 14 Gt Peter Street   **The Office of the Episcopal Church**
London SW1P 3NQ   **in Jerusalem & the Middle East**

September 19, 1980

To his eminence the Ayatollaholuzma Ruhollah Moosavi Khomainy—leader of the Revolution and founder of the Islamic Republic of Iran.

Before the fruition of the Revolution, during Christmas 1978, while still in Paris, you sent a message in the form of a bulletin to all Christians, inviting them to co-operate in the cause of the Revolution. The Diocese of Iran, which is part of the Episcopal Church in Jerusalem and the Middle East also received copies of the same. The Church in Iran, which for its part had experienced the pressures and limitations of the previous regime and interferences by the SAVAK in Church matters, held this message as a good omen. With hopeful hearts, we announced our solidarity with the aims of the Revolution which had vowed to put an end to injustice, bringing freedom, equality, and justice for all, especially religious minorities.

It is now over a year and a half since then and unfortunately, what has befallen the Episcopal Church in Iran within this period, has proved contrary to your promises. The hope for more freedom and justice has turned into disillusion and if the evil, injustice and cruelty against us is not remedied, the shameful mark will remain forever on those responsible.

At first, it was assumed that a small group of opportunists were seeking to take advantage of the situation, with personal benefits and a thirst for power as their only motivations. But evil and cruelty have extended so far that unfortunately, it seems that this small group is being guided and supported by stronger and more dangerous hands for mysterious purposes. These evil-doers have completely forgotten about human values of any kind, blackening the name of the Church in a most dishonourable manner by persecuting, killing, imprisoning, and bringing false accusations against Christians and church workers. They use the media as a means to express anything that comes to their unhealthy minds about us.

Their deeds and words reveal neither any fear of God nor any shame of mankind. They impertinently insist that black is white and white is black, and there is no one to remind them of a line by Sa'adi which reads:

Oh thou who art unjust and cruel
How long dost thou think this can go on?

Instigating the minds and emotions of people against their fellow-men by creating forged documents, false accusations, and causing suspicion is one of the greatest sins in all religions; and yet these cruel people do not even believe in their own Holy Book which warns them against it in verse twelve of the forty-ninth Surah:

O you who are believers
Keep clear of false supposition altogether.

The deeds of these oppressors, namely forging

93

documents, causing suspicion, bringing false accusations and charges of spying against the Episcopal Church in Iran, demonstrate the peak of ingratitude and sacreligion. The Episcopal Church in Iran has served the poor and oppressed for over a century.

What has befallen our small community by the hands of this group and their collaborators has affected ordinary people all over the world, especially Christians of all denominations, to such a degree, that their previous high hopes about the Revolution have sadly given way to the darkest pessimism.

The ugly and treacherous act of forging documents has been carried out so unprofessionally that it doesn't take an expert to notice it. Anyone with a slight knowledge of foreign languages can immediately detect the mistakes, both in spelling and in the whole composition of the documents; thus pointing to the forgery as well as the forgers.

Instead of wasting energy on inventing these false stories about spy charges, how much better it would be if they could think seriously of ways to combat and uproot cruelty and injustice. As the Hadith goes: A state can live without belief, but not without justice.

The Ayatollah, who has himself resisted injustice and cruelty for many years, knows full well that the spreading of lies, false rumours, accusations, and forging documents may deceive simple people for a short while; but wise people do know the truth and in any case no one can deceive God the Omnipotent. Those who believe in God know that in the end truth will prevail and overcome falsehood.

Although I have protested many a time against the cruelties and injustices towards the Episcopal Church in Iran, I am taking this opportunity to proclaim again that all accusations brought against me personally, and against the workers and members of the Episcopal Church in Iran are totally untrue, and the existing documents, some of which have been published, are undoubtedly forged. Thus, officially and with the utmost clarity, I deny all accusations, and summon to court the forgers and those responsible for destroying the rights of the church.

Finally, in order to show the extent of violence and cruelty against the church, I will list the following incidents:

19 February 1979
The murder of the Pastor in charge of churches in the Fars Province, in his office in Shiraz.

11 June 1979
Confiscation of the Christian hospital in Isfahan after over a century of service.

12 July 1979
Confiscation of the Christian hospital in Shiraz and intrusion on church property.

12 August 1979
Confiscation of the Christoffel Blind Mission, belonging to the church.

19 August 1979
Raiding the Bishop's House and Diocesan Offices in Isfahan, and the looting and burning of documents and personal effects.

3 October 1979
Illegal confiscation of the farm for the training of the blind in Isfahan, belonging to the church.

8 October 1979
Disregarding the sanctity of the church, and my pointless and humiliating arrest in Isfahan.

26 October 1979
Attacking the Bishop's House in Isfahan, an attempt on my life and the wounding of my wife, in our bedroom.

1 May 1980
Savage attack on Miss Jean Waddell, the fifty-eight-year-old secretary to the Diocese, and severely wounding her in Tehran.

6 May 1980
The assassination of my only son, twenty-four-year-old Bahram Dehqani-Tafti, on the way back from his college to his mother in Tehran.

5 August 1980
Recalling Miss Jean Waddell from Tehran to Isfahan and her arrest.

9 August 1980
The arrest of Dimitri Bellos, the Diocesan Administrator, in Tehran.

9 August 1980
The expelling of three women in Tehran, who had been responsible for blind work in Isfahan.

10 August 1980
The arrest of Dr and Mrs Coleman in Tehran.

17 August 1980
The arrest of the pastor in charge of St Luke's church in Isfahan.

20 August 1980
The arrest of the pastor in charge of St Andrew's church in Kerman.

In addition to the above-mentioned, a large amount of money belonging to the church has been taken from the banks by force, without permission of any kind; while the rents for seven schools and other church properties have not been paid for a long time. As is clear from the above list, the persecution of church members and the illegal confiscation of church properties started in the first week of the Revolution and still continues relentlessly.

Therefore, I humbly ask you to intervene so that

96

persecution may stop, redress may be made, and above all, six loyal church workers and members who have been held under false and absurd accusations, against all justice and human values in every religion, may be set free, so that the dark clouds which have appeared between Islam and Christianity may be cleared.

Help and grace come from God
and in Him we trust.

H. B. DEHQANI-TAFTI
President of the Episcopal Church in Jerusalem and the Middle East and Bishop in Iran

c.c. Dr Bani-Sadr, the President
Mr Mohammad Ali Rajai, the Prime Minister

I have never received an acknowledgement of the letter, nor of my other protests. All I know is that now ordinary church members are being arrested in Isfahan and Tehran. Seldom in history can it have been that suspicion, misunderstanding, fanaticism, and cupidity have struck an innocent group of people the way they have struck the tiny Episcopal Church in Iran under the Islamic Revolution.

It is time that the story of this persecution should be made known to the world, in the hope that one day justice may be done.

Postscript

As this book was going to press, news came that the Archbishop of Canterbury's special representative, Mr. Terry Waite, had visited Iran and had been able to see and talk with all the Anglican detainees. It was also announced that the Iranian authorities had agreed that they would soon be released, and that the accusations of spying laid against them had been shown to be false.

9

'Truly Life is but Belief and Struggle'

The title of this chapter is one of the sayings of Imam Hussain, revered in the Shi'ite tradition as Lord of the Martyrs—a man who believed in what he said, and who died for his belief. The words were frequently quoted in the early writings of the Revolution. Once I saw them written decoratively on the rear windscreen of a car in Tehran. In Arabic, the slogan consists of only five words, short and to the point: *Innal Hyat Aqidaton va Jahadon.* They much impressed me when I went back to Iran after the Lambeth Conference, with the idea of martyrdom gnawing at my mind.

One of the last ceremonies I had attended in Canterbury Cathedral had been a service to commemorate modern Christian martyrs. I knew of course that martyrdom is not a thing of the past; it can happen anywhere, at any time. But it was somehow different to see in print a list of names of actual people who have been martyred in recent times—names like Dietrich Bonhoeffer and Janani Luwum. Some words of T. S. Eliot, also printed on the service programme, struck me forcibly and have remained part of me ever since: 'A Christian martyrdom is never an accident . . . A martyrdom is always the design of God, for His love of men, to warn them and to lead them, to bring them back to His ways . . .' If I remember rightly, instead of 'the design of God', the programme had 'the gift of God', which to my mind is a better rendering.

So, when the Revolution came, martyrdom was very much in the air. Streets and squares in Iranian cities were renamed after famous martyrs, and actual sites were designated martyrs' memorials.

It was impossible not to respect the courage, zeal, and faith of those who, believing in Imam Hussain's words, actually laid down their lives for the Revolution. We knew that we Christians could not do less; in fact, we were called to do more, to be prepared to be martyred if necessary with love and pity in our hearts, rather than anger and hatred.

But—martyred by whom? We did not know then. One thing we were sure of, that to stand for truth and justice without denying our faith would involve suffering, and perhaps would cost us our lives. It is an irony of the human predicament, a sign of man's waywardness and weakness, that two groups of people can believe equally that 'life is but belief and struggle', yet one of those groups is prepared to persecute the other. It was a tragedy that the Muslim fanatics, struggling as they believed for the preservation of their own faith, could not recognize that a small minority of their fellow-countrymen, while respecting the sincerity of Islam, would in the struggle for justice, truth, and freedom be ready to die for their own belief, that the God of Love was manifested in Jesus Christ.

The Revolution shouted loudly about justice, freedom, and security for all; and there were many who would have done their utmost to bring about a genuinely just, free, and secure society. But the extreme fanatics took over. They became blinded to the fact, and managed to blind others to it, that justice and freedom are indivisible. You cannot unjustly steal property belonging to a church and claim to be just. You cannot frighten people from going to worship and call it freedom. You cannot forge false documents and slander innocent people, ambush and murder their young men, and call it freedom. If you do, your revolution has gone wrong, you yourself have become the oppressor, even if without realizing it. The pity of it was, that by giving in to the fanatics, the revolutionaries lost the sympathy of many moderate, well-educated Iranians who had the cause of a just and free society at heart, thereby depriving the Revolution of the intellectual leadership and experience which any system needs to be truly successful in today's world.

As for the Christians, our service to our country was this: we stood for truth and justice, hoping that the revolutionaries would thereby be brought to recognize their own injustice. We willingly became partakers in the sufferings of Christ, so that some healing might flow into the wounded souls of our people. Our numbers were not large; but when it comes to the most sublime things of life, numbers do not really matter. Some people were helped. A Muslim friend told me how he and others had been encouraged by our stand for truth and justice.

One of the miracles of this life is how God uses very ordinary people, sometimes below average by human standards, to do great things for him. This is the normal way in which he acts. He picks up a man, gives him training in his special ways, and then if he responds, he uses him in most extraordinary ways. From every human point of view, Moses was the last person to liberate the children of Israel from slavery. He had run away from the king's court, he had killed an Egyptian, he stuttered when he spoke; and yet the Lord said to him: 'I will send you to Pharaoh and you shall bring my people Israel out of Egypt.' Moses was appalled by the commission. 'But who am I,' he said to God, 'that I should go to Pharaoh . . .?' God's answer was: 'I am with you.' (Exod. 3.10–12). That was enough. God had chosen him for the purpose, and no matter what his weaknesses, God would be with him.

From childhood I had felt that God had chosen me to serve his church in my own country, because he is the kind of God who chooses 'things low and contemptible, mere nothings' for his purposes to shame the standards of this world (1 Cor. 1.26–29). Now the great test of my life had arrived. I was about to be engulfed by waves much bigger and stronger than myself. How was I prepared for them, and how would I meet their onslaught?

The one thing that was clear to me at this time was my own utter helplessness and weakness. I wrote in my diary:

Sometimes I feel so small, so weak, near to nonentity; and the task is so gigantic and full of awe that I am tempted to regard the whole thing as unreal. But then I hear the voice of God telling me that it is his work. The weaker you are, the stronger his power; and miracles the more possible.

Christians receive from God the power to carry out their mission in life. They get this power through prayer. I have always found prayer difficult, but I have never given it up completely. My main difficulty has always been lack of concentration. I once had the privilege, with some others, of visiting a famous monk, known as Matthew the Poor, who lives in one of the ancient monasteries in the deserts of Egypt. Unwell though he was, he came out of his room to see us, and I took the opportunity to ask him about concentration. He pointed out that concentration relates to the whole of life. A man who is normally a scatter-brain cannot suddenly switch off all the noises within him and achieve full concentration. He has to learn the art of perpetual inner silence.

I greatly benefited, about a year before the Revolution, from a course of twelve tape-recorded talks on meditation, sent to Paul Hunt from England by his sister Jane. They had been prepared by John Main, a Benedictine father, for a Roman Catholic lay foundation known as the Grail. The basis of the technique is to sit in silence twice a day, each time for not less than twenty minutes, repeating to oneself a short phrase from the Bible. Though I found this simplified the problem of concentration, it did not make it easier; indeed real simplicity is always difficult to achieve. But at least I learned where I was; and I continued to persevere, sitting in solitude and repeating what Father Main calls a 'mantra', a word borrowed from Indian religious tradition.

I now believe that God was teaching me this method of meditation to help prepare me to face the oncoming storm. One of the things it did was to bring me face to face with myself. It worked like a vacuum cleaner, drawing out of my inner being everything that was consciously untrue. More and more, I came to realize what Shakespeare meant when he wrote: 'This above all, to thine own self be true.' Unless you are true to yourself, you cannot face difficulties and sufferings creatively.

The breaking waves will soon overwhelm the man who does not know where he is with himself. Calamities will soon bring to their knees those who have had no chance of searching their inner persons in many hours of silence before God. It is true that God is beyond us, outside us; he is what theologians call the transcendent God. But it is also true that the same God is within us; he is the immanent God. He is, as our mystics in Persia have said long ago (and recently Western writers have made the term fashionable), the ground of our existence. In order to find him there, and to establish contact with him within our souls, we have to spend time, we have to be attentive. As we learn to gaze at him with the single eye of complete absorption, we find him there at the rock bottom of our souls—the Rock of our Salvation. Is not this the meaning of 'How blest are those whose hearts are pure; they shall see God' (Matt. 5.8)? Purity of heart means having the house of our being cleansed from all which is not God; then we can face anything in life.

God uses every opportunity to train us, to give us experience of himself, and to prepare us for what lies ahead. Thus, while I am sure he does not wish us to be ill, if we do become unwell he can use the occasion to teach us new things. About three months after the Revolution, just after the assassination of Pastor Syah, I was struck by a mysterious fever, which went up and down for nearly three weeks. No one ever discovered what the cause was; some people thought it was brought on by worry. But the three weeks I spent in bed during those crucial days were of great importance to me. They gave me plenty of time to ponder and to think out a strategy in case things should become worse—as they did.

One thing became clearer than ever to me as I lay thinking about the future. We Christians would have to remain true to our faith no matter what the cost. Not for us the policy of 'tactical dissimulation' (*taqieyh*) which from the early days of Islam the Shi'ite religious leaders have allowed for their followers. *Taqieyh* meant that, if it was dangerous for the Shi'ite Muslim to reveal his real feelings about his faith, he could tactically conceal them. Sa'adi, one of our greatest poets, has done the nation a further disservice with one of his most famous sayings, that 'a benevolent lie is better than a mischievous truth'. All languages have sayings like that—even English uses the term 'a white lie'. But this saying of Sa'adi, coupled with the doctrine of *taqieyh*, has had a most unfortunate effect on our people over the centuries. No doubt the early religious leaders meant well, wanting to save their followers, who were often in the minority, from persecution. Sa'adi was merely telling a story in which the sentence about the 'benevolent lie' occurs. But as so often happens, it has become misused, so much so that often among your so-called friends, you can never be sure where you are with them.

The art of hiding your real intentions, and sometimes pretending to the contrary, has thus become part of Iranian life, affecting the relationship between people and government. For instance, if the people regard it as their religious duty not to obey the law, they will pretend to obey, while in fact ignoring it. These vices of hypocrisy and pretence, prevalent among all peoples on earth, must be combated in order to have healthy and happy societies. I realize that it is here that the

103

Christian church has something positive to offer. There is no doctrine of tactical dissimulation in Christianity. Christ was almost ruthless about being and showing who you are.

'Anyone who wishes to be a follower of mine must leave self behind; he must take up his cross, and come with me. Whoever cares for his own safety is lost; but if a man will let himself be lost for my sake and for the gospel, that man is safe' (Mark 8.34–5). Christians have often been far from obeying this, but whenever they have gone astray, the teachings of Christ and of the Church have been there to remind them.

I saw that we, the Church, must go on as usual, not heeding the threatening signs. We had to be true to what we had discovered to be our true selves. We must take this teaching of Christ literally: 'What does a man gain by winning the whole world at the cost of his true self? What can he give to buy that self back?' (Mark 8.36–37).

A book which was a great help to me on this subject (on which I had often preached) was the play about the life of Thomas More, *A Man for All Seasons* by Robert Bolt. Strangely enough, the book has been translated into Persian—a good translation, by a Muslim. The way Thomas More stood up for what his true self believed to be right, and did not yield to King Henry's pressures, was a great inspiration to me.

When one is ill for a relatively long time, one's mind naturally touches the boundaries of death. During my illness I was reading the diary of a Christian Indian priest, written in hospital during his last illness. His thoughts were pure and lovely. As I read, life and death seemed to me to become one—a straight line starting suddenly and then disappearing into the unknown clouds. It came to me that death is a gift from God, that when it comes one has to accept it with gratitude, and not with terror and fear, because it is only through death that we can be really and completely liberated from our twisted personalities.

One day I had a visitor from Shiraz. He was a Mr S., a convert from Islam, who had been baptized by Pastor Syah; but he had since turned against him and against the church. From what I knew of him, he appeared to be a schizophrenic. I believe that day he either wanted to warn me of a plan that his friends had to assassinate me, or he just wanted to frighten me. He brought a mysterious parcel with him, which he left outside my bedroom before coming in. Then he seated himself in a chair opposite me and put his right hand in his coat pocket, pointing it at me, as if it were a revolver. While he talked about, of all things, the possibility of offering himself as a candidate for ordination, his eyes were rolling all over the place, while his attention seemed fixed on his revolver-shaped hand in his pocket—no wonder my temperature would not come down!

Even in this strange incident, I believe that God was preparing me to meet the worst.

Soon after I had recovered from my illness, I wrote in my diary:

Fear of being killed? In these past few months, especially since Syah's assassination, naturally the thought has occurred to us that there may be assassins after our lives too. The shadowy people who appear and disappear around our dwelling places, ambiguous telephone calls and mysterious messages make us think. It is good to be cautious; but extremely dangerous to let fear take over . . . In these few days I have found out in a clear way that I have to leave fear behind, and carry on with my duties as usual. Of course, if there are people who want to kill me, they will do so. But if God wants me to live, I will survive. The important thing is not to escape from danger and to live, but to continue God's work with utmost loyalty till the end. Today is our twenty-seventh wedding anniversary, and I am in the fifty-ninth year

of my life. Recently I was in bed for three weeks. From one point of view sudden death inflicted by others will be a gift which will save me from the weakness and sufferings of old age. Therefore fear is out of place; it only prevents efficiency. Therefore, O God, enflame thy spirit within me so that alive or dead I may be a witness to thee and for thee.
Isfahan, 6 June 1979.

A few days later, after the expropriation of our properties, I wrote:

These days we are all naturally very worried. But we must keep calm. I am certain that thousands around the world are praying for us. The hairs of our heads are counted. Even one sparrow won't fall down without our Heavenly Father's permission. 'Do not be afraid! It is I!' God is in all the events. We must keep calm and fix our eyes on him, and not worry about the possessions and properties of the church. We must carry on our duties calmly and quietly. We must be humble in front of truth and justice; but we must strongly resist any lawless and unjust act and stand up to any kind of oppression. This is both for the sake of Christianity and Islam, and the Revolution. Neither of these two religions permits oppression and taking other peoples' properties by force. Therefore in order to save Islam and the Revolution from getting a bad name, and to prevent Christianity from the accusation of complacency, we must resist gently and quietly. We have to continue with our protests and try to stand up for truth. We should always have as our aim, faith, hope, and love, and should try to avoid hatred and disharmony. If there is hatred from one side, we must not let it increase and be from both sides.

The fanatics had used intimidation on the other churches to disown us. I am sorry to say that some of them yielded to pressure and openly disclaimed any connection with us, even though they had made use of our institutions and enjoyed happy relationships with us in the past. But the Roman Catholics continued to offer us their friendship and practical support. After Pastor Syah's assassination a group of Catholics in Tehran prepared for us two sets of slides with accompanying tapes on the theme of our Lord with his disciples on Lake Galilee. We used these slides and tapes many times in our services and were comforted and strengthened by them.

When Archbishop William Barden, the head of the Dominican Fathers in Tehran, was finally expelled from the country, the reason given was that he was friendly with the Anglicans! I was very touched to receive a letter on that occasion from Mgr Bugniny, the Papal Nonciatore in Tehran, written in his delightful Italianate English:

> . . . One of the accusations for expelling Mgr Barden was his presence and speech in the burial of your dear son. I wrote clearly to my superiors that the participation at Isfahan to this ceremony was concordated by Mgr Barden with me, and if Mgr Barden would be impossibilitated to go to Isfahan, myself would be gone. Because we are Christians, and if our fraternal love is not in practice demonstrated in these occasions, when will it be?
>
> For your information and consolation in constant friendship.   A. BUGNINY

Such friendships meant a great deal to us; just as signs of alienation from other Christian brethren hurt us very much. Of course, the ancient Orthodox Churches in the Middle East are in a very difficult situation. They have learned over the centuries to live with Islam by not being 'evangelistic', and so in times of persecution they naturally shun fellowship with churches such as ours. This was, I believe, one of the reasons why the World Council of Churches would not officially put the persecution of our Church on the agenda of their Central Committee.

God's timing is always so exact! On Sunday 7 October 1979, the day before they came to arrest me and take me before the Revolutionary Committee, Paul Hunt preached a sermon which was to sustain me during my detention and all through the subsequent events. Speaking of the presence of Christ with us at the time of danger, he quoted a passage from Evelyn Underhill's *The Light of Christ*:

> Look at this picture. You see the stormy lake and the little boat with its low freeboard and shallow draught, just as used on the Lake of Galilee now, and the frightened faces of the fishermen. And standing above them the solitary and tranquil figure of Christ ruling the storm; more than that, for through and in that storm He is revealed to them as never before.
>
> We never realize that power in full until we too are caught and threatened by the violence and hostility of events or the frightful storms of our own unstable natures. It is then that His mysterious action is felt within the circumstances of our lives . . .
>
> 'And He went up unto them into the ship; and the wind ceased: and they were sore amazed . . .'
>
> . . . We do feel sometimes as if we are left to ourselves to struggle with it all. He is away praying on the mountain, or He is asleep in the boat; the waves seem to be getting decidedly higher, the night is very dark and we don't feel sure about our gear—we begin to lose our nerve for life and no one seems to mind. Certainly life is not made soft for Christians; but it is, in the last resort, safe. The universe is safe for souls. The disciples were thoroughly frightened, exhausted, soaked to the skin, but *not* destroyed. At the critical moment He went up into the ship and restored safety, sanity and peace . . . so Christ stands over against history and in its darkest and most dangerous moments we receive a new revelation of His power . . .

So, as I awaited arrest the next morning, in the Bishop

Thompson Memorial Chapel adjacent to our house, I was enabled to write:

Monday 8 October 1979

The Day of Testing

They are coming this morning.

For about an hour now I have been in this chapel, having fellowship with God. I feel his presence within me, about me and in this particular problem and all the present problems in our country and in the world. Everything is in his hand and he is the Just Governor and the Almighty God. Therefore this is my prayer: 'O God, I thank you for the small seed of faith which you have planted in me. According to when it is necessary make that seed grow in strength; give me trust and serenity of heart so that I may be a worthy representative for you. Grant me courage, honesty and fearlessness that I may not show any weakness, except the weakness of the Cross, i.e. loving to the end in the face of hatred and misunderstanding, and perseverance to bear suffering. O God, help me to bear it.

I know that you exist, in me and about me and in these problems. Therefore I will go forward in your Name and surrender to you my dear ones, Margaret, Shirin, Bahram, Sussi, and Guli. Also the church and my fellow workers: F. N., Dimitri, Jean, Iraj, and Paul. Let your will be done!

The day after, I wrote:

Yesterday I wrote about the Day of Testing. Today I will write and say that once more it is proved to me that God exists, in me, about me, and in all the events. If only I surrender everything to him, not worry, and not interfere with his plans, he himself is the Almighty and will end up everything to his glory. Praise be to God!

Thus in so many ways I was prepared by God and by my friends for the worst; so that the attack on my life, when it did come, did not seem to me to be so very shattering. I quote again from my diary, the day after the incident:

It was a strange event. It could only be called a miracle. As far as Margaret and I are concerned, it is obvious to us that God still needs us in this world. Christ is walking on the waters of this world and he has called us to walk with him too. We are walking next to him, albeit shakingly, without any support except himself. Whenever we sink, he will hold us. As long as he wants us to serve him in this world not a single hair will be lost from our heads without his permission. O God, make our faith stronger and stronger and give us humility so that we may serve you in the way of the Cross.
Isfahan, 27 October 1979.

Throughout the ups and downs of the Revolution, with all the uncertainties, the cruelties, the hair-raising experiences, we have found that God's light, his presence within, and his words in the Bible, have guided us, encouraged us, and strengthened us. All we had to do was to be ready to wait on him humbly and quietly, and listen to what he was saying to us.

What of the future?

'Then indeed his voice shook the earth,' writes the author of the Epistle to the Hebrews, and continues: 'Yet once again I will shake not earth alone, but the heavens also . . . The shaking of these created things means their removal, and then what is not shaken will remain . . .' (Heb. 12.26,27).

Some people with whom I have spoken appear to think that the Episcopal Church in Iran is finished. I know it is not. It is true, perhaps, that we shall no longer have our hospitals and schools. 'The shaking of these' has meant 'their removal' from our hands, though

I hope and believe that once things are settled in our country, once the fever of unreasonableness cools down, we shall see justice done. For the sake of law and order we shall ask for some kind of mutual agreement to be signed between the Episcopal Church and a responsible, law-abiding government.

But from the Church's point of view, 'what is not shaken will remain', and that is the disinterested love and service of so many servants of the Church, both Iranian and expatriate, during the one hundred years of the history of the diocese. I cannot believe that such sacrificial love will ever be wasted. Whatever people may say, I know for myself that many men and women missionaries spent the best part of their lives in the service of my country and my people and our church; and if God is the God of love, life, and order, as I believe he is, something of what they tried to build will remain. I do not believe that Pastor Syah's blood was shed in vain. I do not believe that Bahram's young and promising life, so cruelly cut short, will not bear fruit. I do not believe that Margaret's extraordinary courage, selfless love, and service and her deep sorrows and sufferings will be without meaning. I do not believe that Iraj, Dimitri, Nussratollah, the Colemans, and Jean suffered the horrors of imprisonment for no purpose. I do not believe that things in future will be as if nobody had suffered.

If 'life is but belief and struggle', we have certainly believed and we have definitely struggled; therefore we have life, and this life will continue. The cross of Jesus Christ, because of the Church's involvement in the past with worldy powers, has often been misunderstood. Instead of being the symbol of suffering and sacrificial love, it has been regarded by some as the symbol of possessions and power. Christians must reverse this, and the only way of doing so is to be ready to suffer for love's sake, in weakness not in power. The only remedy for a false view of the cross is the cross

111

itself. Even if only a few remain in our church in Iran who believe this, there will still be life, and where life is, there is hope; and more than a few have remained. I should like to end this book with some words I wrote from Iran to my friends overseas in August 1979. They remain as true today as when they were first written.

We have come to understand the book of Job in a new way—'the whirlwind has swept across from the desert and has struck the four corners of the house'. We are learning to say, 'The Lord gives and the Lord takes away, blessed be the name of the Lord.'

At the beginning of the story, when Satan poetically makes a deal with Yahweh, the Jerusalem Bible has it: 'Very well,' Yahweh said to Satan, 'All he has is in your power, but keep your hands off his person!' (Job.1.12). We certainly feel that our 'person', our 'soul', is safe in the hand of Yahweh himself. We have been saved from self-pity which could have destroyed our souls and persons. The way of the Cross has suddenly become so meaningful that we have willingly walked in it with our Lord near us. Never before have we been so optimistic about the future of the Church in our land as we are now! Our numbers have become smaller, our earthly supports have gone, but we are learning the meaning of the faith in a new and deeper way. The shadows of the institutions, like big trees, have gone, their roots are drying up, and now we have the chance of seeing the seed gradually grow in the light of the sun, and sending its roots deep down into the indigenous soil.

The end of an era has clearly come and with it the beginning of a new one. May we be given the faith, hope, courage, humility, insight, wisdom, love, and perseverance, to obey the call we have had from God in the way our predecessors carried on with theirs, in this new situation in the world of today.

A Father's Prayer
upon the Murder of his Son

O God,

We remember not only Bahram but also his murderers;

Not because they killed him in the prime of his youth and made our hearts bleed and our tears flow,

Not because with this savage act they have brought further disgrace on the name of our country among the civilized nations of the world;

But because through their crime we now follow thy footsteps more closely in the way of sacrifice.

The terrible fire of this calamity burns up all selfishness and possessiveness in us;

Its flame reveals the depth of depravity and meanness and suspicion, the dimension of hatred and the measure of sinfulness in human nature;

It makes obvious as never before our need to trust in God's love as shown in the cross of Jesus and his resurrection;

Love which makes us free from hate towards our persecutors;

Love which brings patience, forbearance, courage, loyalty, humility, generosity, greatness of heart;

Love which more than ever deepens our trust in God's final victory and his eternal designs for the Church and for the world;

Love which teaches us how to prepare ourselves to face our own day of death.

O God.

Bahram's blood has multiplied the fruit of the Spirit in the soil of our souls;

So when his murderers stand before thee on the day of judgement

Remember the fruit of the Spirit by which they have enriched our lives,

And forgive.

Glossary

Ayatollah	lit. a sign of God, a title given to leading Islamic divines
Azan	the call to prayer
Fuqaha	jurists skilled in Islamic law, or Muslim theologians
Hadith	A saying or tradition of the prophet Mohammed or of the Imams
Hakem-e shar'	the leading Shi'ite judge or authority
Hujatol-Islam	lit. a proof of Islam, a title given to leading *ulama*
Majlis	the national consultative assembly
Muezzin	the one who gives the call to prayer
Mujtahid	one duly qualified to give a ruling on religious matters
Mullah	one of the lesser *ulama*
Qur'an	the record of the sayings of God revealed to Mohammed
Shi'a, Shi'ite	Islam is divided into two main sects, the Sunni and the Shi'ite. The Shi'a is the sect which believes that Mohammed designated Ali as his successor in the headship of the community and that thereafter it passed in succession to twelve of his descendants by his wife Fatima, each of whom was *Imam*. The twelfth *Imam* disappeared and has since remained in occultation. Those who belong to the Shi'a are known as Shi'is or Shi'ites.
Surah	a chapter or section of the Qur'an
Ulama	men learned in the religious law
Waqf	land immobilized for a charitable object

115

Acknowledgements

I wish to thank my publishers, the Society for Promoting Christian Knowledge, for their close co-operation in the writing of this book. Particularly I would like to thank Miss Myrtle Powley, Editor of Triangle Books, for her patience in going through the manuscript with me.

I am also grateful to Professor A. K. S. Lambton, D. Litt., for her advice and help in preparing the Glossary.

The poem by Michael Burn, quoted on page 87 is reproduced by kind permission of the writer.

The passage from *The Light of Christ* by Evelyn Underhill, quoted on page 108, is reproduced by permission of Longman Ltd.

All biblical quotations, unless otherwise indicated, are from the New English Bible, second edition © 1970, and are quoted by permission of the Oxford and Cambridge University Presses.